The Complete 5-Ingredient Keto Diet Cookbook

Cookbook

Simple and Easy Recipes for Busy People
on Ketogenic Diet with 2-Week Meal Plan

Andrew Ross

CONTENTS

PORK, BEEF & LAMB RECIPES...34

SEAFOOD & FISH RECIPES 49

INTRODUCTION

Understanding the craze of the Ketogenic Diet

I'll tell you. Long before we got all "richly" about meals – I mean loading our plates with meats, cheeses, and creamy goodness; the folks dating back from 500 BC were already on this spree.

To them, they left carbohydrates out of their diets to treat epilepsy in children and ate foods with high fats,proteins, and many green vegetables. And guess what? It worked!

This is what the Ketogenic Diet is, removing high carbs from foods and eating high fats and proteins instead. It solves a diverse range of ailments by merely reducing the amounts of sugars in the body and allowing good fats play a healing role.

Usually, the body will "lazily" burn energy from carbohydrates because it is easiest while fats, which are supposed to be burned for energy, sit in the body and do nothing. Because they lay idle, your love handles keep increasing, your cheeks get plumper, and you find fats in all the areas of your body that you will rather prefer that they weren't.

Thanks to the many researchers that dug out this ancient secret, it is a diet for now and for the future. Having been embraced by many medical practitioners and healthy living enthusiasts, it is of no surprise that the Ketogenic Diet is one of the first recommendations for curing varying ailments – this is how far good craze has gone.

For me, it is a feel-good kind of a diet. It keeps me sane, light-weighted, and feeling fresh within and out; I couldn't ask for more.

THE KETOGENIC DIET

The positives of the Ketogenic Diet

Blood Sugar Control

Starchy foods and sugary foods produce sugars in the body. This is why people with diabetes suffer, and to my surprise, in the past, meal plans created for people with diabetes were loaded with carbohydrates, fruits, and processed milk. So wrong!

By avoiding carbohydrates, the amount of sugars in the body drops drastically, which requires a relative reduction in the use of diabetic medication.

Significant enough, there are many testimonies of the Keto diet healing diabetics completely; that's some good news right there!

Weight loss

It goes without stressing that you're up for a significant weight shed once you start dieting the Keto way. Why so? Because your body now burns all the stored up fat in your body for energy.

Like I said earlier when on carbs, the body's duty to consume fats gets dormant and will rather burn carbs. But, when carbohydrates are reduced, the body is moved into a metabolic state called ketosis where it is forced to burn fats.

Appetite Control

Ever wondered why there is a word as "sweet-tooth"? The more sugars you eat, the more of it you will want. Therefore, the unexpected hunger pangs after taking sugary foods or fruits.

Appetite levels increase, not necessarily, because the body needs food. It is because the body burns sugars fast and creates a false alert that it needs more food.The truth is it just needs some SUGAR.

On the keto diet, fat burns slower keeping the body fuller for an extended period. I usually find myself eating twice a day on a healthy meal because my breakfast is fat-rich and keeps me full past my lunch period sometimes.

If hungry in between meals, I snack on a Keto option, and I'm good.

Energy Levels

Starch and sugars are tricky – they satisfy fast, but burn out fast. When this happens, the body is left weak and craves more carbs only to be burned quickly again. Energy levels then fluctuate causing most parts of the body to be less vibrant.

On the other hand, feeding on high fats and Proteins create a steady level of energy because fats and Protein burn gradually and in a consistent manner.

Keto Diet and Insulin Resistance

On a high carb diet, the body breaks starch into useful sugar components known as glucose, which is transported to the muscles and tissues as energy. The carrier of this glucose is insulin – meant to be a good thing.

However, in cases where the body becomes resistant to insulin, sugar breaks lose in the body. Once, the liver, cells in the muscles, and fats stop absorbing the sugars, they find their way into the blood and have a free flow – diabetes sets in.

Through the Keto diet, this problem is prevented because the body is naturally reduced of sugars through carb reduction hence there is more control over the amount of sugar needed in the body.

Why fats and Proteins – does this mean carbohydrates are bad?

No, don't get it twisted. Carbohydrates aren't bad for the sense that they are nature's gift for feeding. However, for their starchy and sugary components, a small measure of carb intake should be considered to avoid increased sugar levels and low energy.

Fats and Pproteins, on the other hand, are safer options to consume in larger quantities. They are a more sustainable way of providing energy to the body, lead to weight loss, and are entirely healthy to the body.

Meanwhile, fats can be categorized into two parts: good and bad fats. Below I give examples of some good fats, but mostly these are sourced from natural ingredients like meat, fatty fish, nuts, avocados, tofu, and seeds. While bad fats are often processed products, for example, some "vegetable oils."

Concisely, you want to ensure that you are deriving your fats from natural sources and using vegetables with low carb counts if you need to eat carbohydrates like rice.

Side effects of the Ketogenic Diet

While it sucks to say that the Keto Diet has its wrong sides, it sure does like every other thing.

Frequent urination

Which is a good thing! Because most edibles are plant-based, the body gathers water quickly resulting in regular use of the washroom.

While it may be discomforting, it is a good way of washing toxins out of the body quickly and more effectively. It leaves the body feeling fresh.

Constipation

At the beginning of the diet, the body may dehydrate due to frequent urination. Also, the increased amount of nuts may harden the contents of the colon resulting in constipation.

In this case, make sure to drink a lot of water, eat a lot of non-starchy vegetables, and take in enough salt to soften the colon's content.

Diabetic Ketoacidosis

For people with diabetes, when the body produces excessive ketones, an adequate production of insulin is short.

The body is then unable to transport the necessary amounts of glucose and sugars to the muscles and tissue, resulting in fatigue, shortness of breath, frequent urination, nausea, and vomiting, etc.

If diabetic, consult a doctor or dietician to help draw out appropriate vegan-keto meal plans to keep you healthy.

Keto Flu

Within the first few days of the keto diet, you are likely to experience flu-like symptoms; headaches, fatigue, dullness, irritability – these are fine. They are just your body's reaction to a change in dieting.

After four days, you will have adjusted to the new diet and feel active and vibrant.

<u>Low Physical Performance</u>

Energy levels may be low at the start since the body is deprived of carbohydrates and sugars. At this point, try not to be involved in high-intensity activities.

In a few days, your energy level will be back up, and you will be more energetic than you were before the diet.

Ask Your Doctor

Finally, you want to speak with your doctor before starting the vegan-keto diet. For pregnant women, health-related reason or if unsure that the keto-veganism is right for you, please talk with your doctor.

This is a safe diet and should technically work well for everyone; however, a little extra caution doesn't hurt.

About the Recipes

IN THIS BOOK YOU WILL FIND SIMPLE AND EASY, 5-INGREDIENT RECIPES FOR EVERY MEAL.

Over half the recipes take less than 30 minutes to prepare, and whenever possible, I tried to minimize the number of pots and pans needed because I love for cleanup to be easy, too.

Each recipe in the book calls for just five main ingredients and uses some of these five pantry ingredients also: pink Himalayan salt, freshly ground black pepper, grass-fed ghee, olive oil, and grass-fed butter.

You'll also find the nutritional information as well as the macro breakdowns at the bottom of each recipe to help you make those notes I spoke about earlier.

Now, ready? Let's get some body-loving started!

SMOOTHIES & BREAKFASTS

Raspberry Chia Pudding

Ready in about: 4 minutes | Serves: 4

INGREDIENTS

2 cups raspberries, reserve a few for topping
3 cups unsweetened vanilla almond milk
1 cup heavy cream

1 cup chia seeds
4 tsp liquid stevia
Chopped mixed nuts for topping

DIRECTIONS

In a medium bowl, crush the raspberries with a fork until pureed.

Pour in with the almond milk, heavy cream, chia seeds, and liquid stevia. Mix and refrigerate the pudding overnight. Spoon the pudding into serving glasses, top with raspberries, mixed nuts, and serve.

NUTRITIONAL INFO PER SERVING: Calories 390, Fat 33.5g, Net Carbs 3g, Protein 13g

Spicy Egg Muffins with Bacon & Cheese

Ready in about: 30 minutes | Serves: 6

INGREDIENTS

12 eggs
¼ cup coconut milk
Salt and black pepper to taste

1 cup grated cheddar cheese
12 slices bacon
4 jalapeños, seeded and minced

DIRECTIONS

Preheat oven to 370ºF.

Crack the eggs into a bowl and whisk with coconut milk until combined, season with salt and pepper, and evenly stir in the cheddar cheese.

Line each hole of a muffin tin with a slice of bacon and fill each with the egg mixture two-thirds way up. Top with the jalapenos and bake in the oven for 18 to 20 minutes or until puffed and golden. Remove, allow cooling for a few minutes, and serve with arugula salad.

NUTRITIONAL INFO PER SERVING: Calories 302, Fat 23.7g, Net Carbs 3.2g, Protein 20g

Ham & Egg Broccoli Bake

Ready in about: 25 minutes | Serves: 4

INGREDIENTS

2 heads broccoli, cut into small florets
2 red bell peppers, seeded and chopped
¼ cup chopped ham
2 tsp ghee

1 tsp dried oregano + extra to garnish
Salt and black pepper to taste
8 fresh eggs

DIRECTIONS

Preheat oven to 425ºF.

Melt the ghee in a frying pan over medium heat; brown the ham, stirring frequently, about 3 minutes.

Arrange the broccoli, bell peppers, and ham on a foil-lined baking sheet in a single layer, toss to combine; season with salt, oregano, and pepper. Bake for 10 minutes until the vegetables have softened.

Remove, create eight indentations with a spoon, and crack an egg into each. Return to the oven and continue to bake for an additional 5 to 7 minutes until the egg whites are firm. Season with salt, pepper, and extra oregano, share the bake into four plates and serve with strawberry lemonade (optional).

NUTRITIONAL INFO PER SERVING: Calories 344, Fat 28g, Net Carbs 4.2g, Protein 11g

Smoked Salmon Rolls with Dill Cream Cheese

Ready in about: 10 minutes + time refrigeration | Serves: 3

INGREDIENTS

3 tbsp cream cheese, softened
1 small lemon, zested and juiced
3 tsp chopped fresh dill

Salt and black pepper to taste
3 (7-inch) low carb tortillas
6 slices smoked salmon

DIRECTIONS

In a bowl, mix the cream cheese, lemon juice, zest, dill, salt, and black pepper.

Lay each tortilla on a plastic wrap (just wide enough to cover the tortilla), spread with cream cheese mixture, and top each (one) with two salmon slices. Roll up the tortillas and secure both ends by twisting.

Refrigerate for 2 hours, remove plastic, cut off both ends of each wrap, and cut wraps into half-inch wheels.

NUTRITIONAL INFO PER SERVING: Calories 250, Fat 16g, Net Carbs 7g, Protein 18g

Italian Sausage Stacks

Ready in about: 16 minutes | Serves: 6

INGREDIENTS

6 Italian sausage patties
4 tbsp olive oil
2 ripe avocados, pitted
2 tsp fresh lime juice

Salt and black pepper to taste
6 fresh eggs
Red pepper flakes to garnish

DIRECTIONS

In a skillet, warm the oil over medium heat and fry the sausage patties about 8 minutes until lightly browned and firm. Put the patties in a plate.

Spoon the avocado into a bowl, mash with the lime juice, and season with salt and black pepper. Spread the mash on the sausages.

Boil 3 cups of water in a wide pan over high heat, and reduce to simmer (don't boil).

Crack each egg into a small bowl and gently put the egg into the simmering water; poach for 2 to 3 minutes. Use a perforated spoon to remove from the water on a paper towel to dry. Repeat with the other 5 eggs. Top each stack with a poached egg, sprinkle with chili flakes, salt, pepper, and chives. Serve with turnip wedges.

NUTRITIONAL INFO PER SERVING: Calories 378, Fat 23g, Net Carbs 5g, Protein 16g

Fontina Cheese and Chorizo Waffles

Ready in about: 30 minutes | Serves: 6

INGREDIENTS

6 eggs
6 tbsp almond milk
1 tsp Spanish spice mix
Sea salt and black pepper, to taste

3 chorizo sausages, cooked, chopped
1 cup fontina cheese, shredded
Cooking spray

DIRECTIONS

Using a mixing bowl, beat the eggs, Spanish spice mix, black pepper, salt, and almond milk. Add in shredded cheese and chopped sausage. Use a nonstick cooking spray to spray a waffle iron.

Cook the egg mixture for 5 minutes. Serve alongside homemade sugar-free tomato ketchup.

NUTRITIONAL INFO PER SERVING: Calories 316; Fat: 25g, Net Carbs: 1.5g, Protein: 20.2g

Breakfast Almond Muffins

Ready in about: 30 minutes | Serves: 4

INGREDIENTS

Cooking spray
2 cups almond flour
2 tsp low carb baking powder
½ tsp salt

8 oz cream cheese, softened
¼ cup melted butter
1 egg
1 cup unsweetened almond milk

DIRECTIONS

Preheat oven to 400ºF and grease a 12-cup muffin tray with cooking spray. Mix the flour, baking powder, and salt in a large bowl.

In a separate bowl, beat the cream cheese and butter using a hand mixer and whisk in the egg and milk. Fold in the flour, and spoon the batter into the muffin cups two-thirds way up.

Bake for 20 minutes until puffy at the top and golden brown, remove to a wire rack to cool slightly for 5 minutes before serving. Serve with tea.

NUTRITIONAL INFO PER SERVING: Calories 320, Fat 30.6g, Net Carbs 6g, Protein 4g

Avocado and Kale Eggs

Ready in about: 20 minutes | Serves: 4

INGREDIENTS

1 tsp ghee
1 red onion, sliced
4 oz chorizo, sliced into thin rounds
1 cup chopped kale

1 ripe avocado, pitted, peeled, chopped
4 eggs
Salt and black pepper to season

DIRECTIONS

Preheat oven to 370ºF. Melt ghee in a cast iron pan over medium heat and sauté the onion for 2 minutes. Add the chorizo and cook for 2 minutes more, flipping once.

Introduce the kale in batches with a splash of water to wilt, season lightly with salt, stir and cook for 3 minutes. Mix in the avocado and turn the heat off.

Create four holes in the mixture, crack the eggs into each hole, sprinkle with salt and black pepper, and slide the pan into the preheated oven and bake for 6 minutes until the egg whites are set or firm but with the yolks still runny.

Adjust the taste with salt and black pepper, and serve right away with low carb toasts.

NUTRITIONAL INFO PER SERVING: Calories 274, Fat 23g, Net Carbs 4g, Protein 13g

Egg Tofu Scramble with Kale & Mushrooms

Ready in about: 30 minutes | Serves: 4

INGREDIENTS

1 tbsp ghee
1 cup sliced white mushrooms
2 cloves garlic, minced
16 oz firm tofu, pressed and crumbled

Salt and black pepper to taste
½ cup thinly sliced kale
6 fresh eggs

DIRECTIONS

Melt the ghee in a non-stick skillet over medium heat, and sauté the mushrooms for 5 minutes until they lose their liquid. Add the garlic and cook for 1 minute.

Crumble the tofu into the skillet, season with salt and pepper. Cook with continuous stirring for 6 minutes. Introduce the kale in batches and cook to soften for about 7 minutes.

Crack the eggs into a bowl, whisk until well combined and creamy in color, and pour all over the kale. Use a spatula to immediately stir the eggs while cooking until scrambled and no more runny, about 5 minutes.

Adjust the taste with salt and pepper, plate, and serve with low carb crusted bread.

NUTRITIONAL INFO PER SERVING: Calories 469, Fat 39g, Net Carbs 5g, Protein 25g

Egg in a Cheesy Spinach Nests

Ready in about: 37 minutes | Serves: 4

INGREDIENTS

1 tbsp olive oil
1 clove garlic, grated
½ lb spinach, chopped
Salt and black pepper to taste
2 tbsp shredded Gouda cheese

2 tbsp shredded Parmesan cheese + some more
Cooking spray
4 eggs

DIRECTIONS

Preheat oven to 350ºF. Warm the oil in a non-stick skillet over medium heat; add the garlic and sauté until softened for 2 minutes. Add the spinach to wilt about 5 minutes and season with salt and black pepper.

Top with Parmesan and Gouda cheeses, sauté for a further 2 minutes and turn the heat off. Allow complete cooling.

Grease a baking sheet with cooking spray, mold 4 (firm & separate) spinach nests on the sheet, and crack an egg into each nest. Season with salt and black pepper, and sprinkle with Parmesan cheese.

Bake for 15 minutes just until the egg whites have set and the yolks are still runny. Plate the nests and serve right away with toasts and coffee.

NUTRITIONAL INFO PER SERVING: Calories 230, Fat 17.5g, Net Carbs 4g, Protein 12g

Baked Eggs in Avocados

Ready in about: 13 minutes | Serves: 4

INGREDIENTS

2 large avocados, halved and pitted
4 eggs

Salt and black pepper to season
Chopped parsley to garnish

DIRECTIONS

Preheat the oven to 400ºF.

Then, crack each egg into each avocado half and place them on a baking sheet.

Bake the filled avocado in the oven for 8 or 10 minutes or until eggs are cooked. Season with salt and pepper, and garnish with parsley.

NUTRITIONAL INFO PER SERVING: Calories 234, Fat 19.1g, Net Carbs 2.2g, Protein 8.2g

Sausage & Squash Omelet with Swiss Chard

Ready in about: 10 minutes | Serves: 1

INGREDIENTS

2 eggs
1 cup swiss chard, chopped
4 oz sausage, chopped
2 tbsp ricotta cheese

4 ounces roasted squash
1 tbsp olive oil
Salt and black pepper, to taste

DIRECTIONS

Beat the eggs in a bowl, season with salt and pepper and stir in the swiss chard and the ricotta.

In another bowl, mash the squash. Add the squash to the egg mixture. Heat ¼ tbsp. of olive oil in a pan over medium heat. Add sausage and cook until browned on all sides, turning occasionally.

Drizzle the remaining olive oil. Pour the egg mixture over. Cook for about 2 minutes per side until the eggs are thoroughly cooked and lightly browned. Remove the pan and run a spatula around the edges of the omelet; slide it onto a warm platter. Fold in half, and serve hot.

NUTRITIONAL INFO PER SERVING: Calories 558, Fat 51.7g, Net Carbs 7.5g, Protein 32.3g

Chorizo and Mozzarella Omelet

Ready in about: 15 minutes | Serves: 1

INGREDIENTS

2 eggs
6 basil leaves
2 ounces mozzarella
1 tbsp butter

1 tbsp water
4 thin slices chorizo
1 tomato, sliced
Salt and black pepper, to taste

DIRECTIONS

Whisk the eggs along with the water and some salt and pepper. Melt the butter in a skillet and cook the eggs for 30 seconds. Spread the chorizo slices over. Arrange the sliced tomato and mozzarella over the chorizo. Cook for about 3 minutes. Cover the skillet and continue cooking for 3 more minutes until omelet is completely set.

When ready, remove the pan from heat; run a spatula around the edges of the omelet and flip it onto a warm plate, folded side down. Serve garnished with basil leaves and a green salad.

NUTRITIONAL INFO PER SERVING: Calories 451, Fat: 36.5g, Net Carbs: 3g, Protein: 30g

Hashed Zucchini & Bacon Breakfast

Ready in about: 25 minutes | Serves: 1

INGREDIENTS

1 medium zucchini, diced
2 bacon slices
1 egg
1 tbsp olive oil

½ small onion, chopped
1 tbsp chopped parsley
¼ tsp salt

DIRECTIONS

Place the bacon in a skillet and cook over medium heat for a few minutes, until the bacon is crispy. Remove from the skillet and set aside.

Warm the olive oil and cook the onion until soft, for about 3-4 minutes, occasionally stirring. Add the zucchini, and cook for 10 more minutes until zucchini is brown and tender, but not mushy. Transfer to a plate and season with salt.

Crack the egg into the same skillet and fry over medium heat. Top the zucchini mixture with the bacon slices and a fried egg. Serve hot, sprinkled with parsley.

NUTRITIONAL INFO PER SERVING: Calories 423, Fat: 35.5g, Net Carbs: 6.6g, Protein: 17.4g

Traditional Spinach and Feta Frittata

Ready in about: 40 minutes | Serves: 4

INGREDIENTS

5 ounces spinach
8 ounces crumbled feta cheese
1 pint halved cherry tomatoes
10 eggs

3 tbsp olive oil
4 scallions, diced
Salt and black pepper, to taste

DIRECTIONS

Preheat your oven to 350ºF.

Drizzle the oil in a 2-quart casserole and place in the oven until heated. In a bowl, whisk the eggs along with the pepper and salt, until thoroughly combined. Stir in the spinach, feta cheese, and scallions.

Pour the mixture into the casserole, top with the cherry tomatoes and place back in the oven. Bake for 25 minutes until your frittata is set in the middle.

When done, remove the casserole from the oven and run a spatula around the edges of the frittata; slide it onto a warm platter. Cut the frittata into wedges and serve with salad.

NUTRITIONAL INFO PER SERVING: Calories 461, Fat: 35g, Net Carbs: 6g, Protein: 26g

Eggs & Crabmeat with Creme Fraiche Salsa

Ready in about: 15 minutes | Serves: 3

INGREDIENTS

1 tbsp olive oil
6 eggs, whisked

1 (6 oz) can crabmeat, flaked
Salt and black pepper to taste

For the Salsa:

¾ cup crème fraiche
½ cup scallions, chopped

Salt and black pepper to the taste
½ tsp fresh dill, chopped

DIRECTIONS

Set a sauté pan over medium-high heat and warm olive oil. Place in eggs and scramble them.

Stir in crabmeat and cook until cooked thoroughly; season with salt and pepper.

In a mixing dish, combine all salsa ingredients. Equally, split the egg/crabmeat mixture among 4 plates; serve alongside the scallions and salsa to the side.

NUTRITIONAL INFO PER SERVING: Calories 334; Fat: 26.2g, Net Carbs: 4.4g, Protein: 21.1g

Quick Blue Cheese Omelet

Ready in about: 15 minutes | Serves: 2

INGREDIENTS

4 eggs
Salt, to taste
1 tbsp sesame oil

½ cup blue cheese, crumbled
1 tomato, thinly sliced

DIRECTIONS

In a mixing bowl, beat the eggs and season with salt.

Set a sauté pan over medium heat and warm oil. Add in the eggs and cook as you swirl the eggs around the pan using a spatula. Cook eggs until partially set. Top with cheese; fold the omelet in half to enclose filling. Decorate with tomato and serve while warm.

NUTRITIONAL INFO PER SERVING: Calories 307; Fat: 25g, Net Carbs: 2.5g, Protein: 18.5g

Cheesy Turkey Sausage Egg Muffins

Ready in about: 10 minutes | Serves: 3

INGREDIENTS

1 tsp butter, melted
6 eggs, separated into yolks and whites
Salt and black pepper, to taste

½ tsp dried rosemary
1 cup pecorino romano cheese, grated
3 turkey sausages, chopped

DIRECTIONS

Set oven to 420ºF. Lightly grease a muffin pan with the melted butter.

Use an electric mixer to beat the egg whites until there is a formation of stiff peaks. Add in sausages, cheese, and seasonings. Add into muffin cups and bake for 4 minutes.

Place in an egg to each of the cups. Bake for an additional of 4 minutes. Allow cooling before serving.

NUTRITIONAL INFO PER SERVING: Calories 423; Fat: 34.1g, Net Carbs: 2.2g, Protein: 26.5g

POULTRY RECIPES

Bacon Wrapped Chicken with Grilled Asparagus

Ready in about: 48 minutes | Serves: 4

INGREDIENTS

6 chicken breasts
8 bacon slices
4 tbsp olive oil
1 lb asparagus spears

Salt and black pepper to taste
2 tbsp fresh lemon juice
Manchego cheese for topping

DIRECTIONS

Preheat the oven to 400ºF.

Season chicken breasts with salt and black pepper, and wrap 2 bacon slices around each chicken breast. Arrange on a baking sheet that is lined with parchment paper, drizzle with oil and bake for 25-30 minutes until bacon is brown and crispy.

Preheat your grill on high heat.

Brush the asparagus spears with olive oil and season with salt. Grill for 8-10 minutes, frequently turning until slightly charred. Remove to a plate and drizzle with lemon juice. Grate over Manchego cheese so that it melts a little on contact with the hot asparagus and forms a cheesy dressing.

NUTRITIONAL INFO PER SERVING: Calories 468, Fat 38g, Net Carbs 2g, Protein 26g

Yummy Chicken Nuggets

Ready in about: 25 minutes | Serves: 2

INGREDIENTS

½ cup almond flour
1 egg
2 tbsp garlic powder

2 chicken breasts, cubed
Salt and black pepper, to taste
½ cup butter

DIRECTIONS

Using a bowl, combine salt, garlic powder, flour, and pepper, and stir. In a separate bowl, beat the egg. Add the chicken breast cubes in egg mixture, then in the flour mixture. Set a pan over medium-high heat and warm butter, add in the chicken nuggets, and cook for 6 minutes on each side. Remove to paper towels, drain the excess grease and serve.

NUTRITIONAL INFO PER SERVING: Calories 417, Fat 37g, Net Carbs 4.3g, Protein 35g

Spinach Chicken Cheesy Bake

Ready in about: 45 minutes | Serves: 6

INGREDIENTS

6 chicken breasts, skinless and boneless
1 tsp mixed spice seasoning
Pink salt and black pepper to season
2 loose cups baby spinach

3 tsp olive oil
4 oz cream cheese, cubed
1 ¼ cups shredded mozzarella cheese
4 tbsp water

DIRECTIONS

Preheat oven to 370ºF.

Season chicken with spice mix, salt, and black pepper. Pat with your hands to have the seasoning stick on the chicken. Put in the casserole dish and layer spinach over the chicken. Mix the oil with cream cheese, mozzarella, salt, and black pepper and stir in water a tablespoon at a time. Pour the mixture over the chicken and cover the pot with aluminium foil.

Bake for 20 minutes, remove foil and continue cooking for 15 minutes until a nice golden brown color is formed on top. Take out and allow sitting for 5 minutes.

Serve warm with braised asparagus.

NUTRITIONAL INFO PER SERVING: Calories 340, Fat 30.2g, Net Carbs 3.1g, Protein 15g

Roasted Stuffed Chicken with Tomato Basil Sauce

Ready in about: 45 minutes | Serves: 6

INGREDIENTS

4 ounces cream cheese
3 oz mozzarella slices
10 ounces spinach
½ cup shredded mozzarella

1 tbsp olive oil
1 cup tomato basil sauce
3 whole chicken breasts

DIRECTIONS

Preheat your oven to 400ºF. Combine the cream cheese, mozzarella slices, and spinach in the microwave.

Cut the chicken with the knife a couple of times horizontally. Stuff with the filling. Brush the top with olive oil. Place on a lined baking dish and in the oven. Bake in the oven for 25 minutes.

Pour the sauce over and top with mozzarella. Return to oven and cook for 5 minutes.

NUTRITIONAL INFO PER SERVING: Calories 338, Fat: 28g, Net Carbs: 2.5g, Protein: 37g

Cilantro Chicken Breasts with Mayo-Avocado Sauce

Ready in about: 22 minutes | Serves: 4

INGREDIENTS

For the Sauce

1 avocado, pitted
½ cup mayonnaise

Salt to taste

For the Chicken

3 tbsp ghee
4 chicken breasts
Pink salt and black pepper to taste

1 cup chopped cilantro leaves
½ cup chicken broth

DIRECTIONS

Spoon the avocado, mayonnaise, and salt into a small food processor and puree until smooth sauce is derived. Adjust taste with salt as desired.

Pour sauce into a jar and refrigerate while you make the chicken.

Melt ghee in a large skillet, season chicken with salt and black pepper and fry for 4 minutes on each side to golden brown. Remove chicken to a plate.

Pour the broth in the same skillet and add the cilantro. Bring to simmer covered for 3 minutes and add the chicken. Cover and cook on low heat for 5 minutes until liquid has reduced and chicken is fragrant. Dish chicken only into serving plates and spoon the mayo-avocado sauce over.

NUTRITIONAL INFO PER SERVING: Calories 398, Fat 32g, Net Carbs 4g, Protein 24g

Lemon & Rosemary Chicken in a Skillet

Ready in about: 1 hour and 20 minutes | Serves: 4

INGREDIENTS

8 chicken thighs
1 tsp salt
2 tbsp lemon juice
1 tsp lemon zest

2 tbsp olive oil
1 tbsp chopped thyme
¼ tsp black pepper
1 garlic clove, minced

DIRECTIONS

Combine all ingredients in a bowl. Place in the fridge for one hour.

Heat a skillet over medium heat. Add the chicken along with the juices and cook until crispy, about 7 minutes per side.

NUTRITIONAL INFO PER SERVING: Calories 477, Fat: 31g, Net Carbs: 2.5g, Protein: 31g

Eggplant & Tomato Braised Chicken Thighs

Ready in about: 45 minutes | Serves: 4

INGREDIENTS

2 tbsp ghee
1 lb chicken thighs
Pink salt and black pepper to taste
2 cloves garlic, minced

1 (14 oz) can whole tomatoes
1 eggplant, diced
10 fresh basil leaves, chopped + extra to garnish

DIRECTIONS

Melt ghee in a saucepan over medium heat, season the chicken with salt and black pepper, and fry for 4 minutes on each side until golden brown. Remove chicken onto a plate.

Sauté the garlic in the ghee for 2 minutes, pour in the tomatoes, and cook covered for 8 minutes.

Add in the eggplant and basil. Cook for 4 minutes. Season the sauce with salt and black pepper, stir and add the chicken. Coat with sauce and simmer for 3 minutes.

Serve chicken with sauce on a bed of squash pasta. Garnish with extra basil.

NUTRITIONAL INFO PER SERVING: Calories 468, Fat 39.5g, Net Carbs 2g, Protein 26g

Lemon Threaded Chicken Skewers

Ready in about: 2 hours 17 minutes | Serves: 4

INGREDIENTS

3 chicken breasts, cut into cubes
2 tbsp olive oil, divided
2/3 jar preserved lemon, flesh removed, drained
2 cloves garlic, minced

½ cup lemon juice
Salt and black pepper to taste
1 tsp rosemary leaves to garnish
2 to 4 lemon wedges to garnish

DIRECTIONS

First, thread the chicken onto skewers and set aside.

In a wide bowl, mix half of the oil, garlic, salt, pepper, and lemon juice, and add the chicken skewers, and lemon rind. Cover the bowl and let the chicken marinate for at least 2 hours in the refrigerator.

When the marinating time is almost over, preheat a grill to 350ºF, and remove the chicken onto the grill. Cook for 6 minutes on each side. Remove and serve warm with a drizzle of tomato sauce. Garnish with rosemary leaves and lemons wedges, and serve with braised asparagus.

NUTRITIONAL INFO PER SERVING: Calories 350, Fat 11g, Net Carbs 3.5g, Protein 34g

Chicken Skewers with Celery Fries

Ready in about: 60 minutes | Serves: 4

INGREDIENTS

2 chicken breasts
½ tsp salt
¼ tsp ground black pepper

2 tbsp olive oil
¼ cup chicken broth

For the fries

1 lb celery root
2 tbsp olive oil

½ tsp salt
¼ tsp ground black pepper

DIRECTIONS

Set an oven to 400ºF. Grease and line a baking sheet. In a large bowl, mix oil, spices and the chicken; set in the fridge for 10 minutes while covered. Peel and chop celery root to form fry shapes and place into a separate bowl. Apply oil to coat and add pepper and salt for seasoning. Arrange to the baking tray in an even layer and bake for 10 minutes.

Take the chicken from the refrigerator and thread onto the skewers. Place over the celery, pour in the chicken broth, then set in the oven for 30 minutes. Serve with lemon wedges.

NUTRITIONAL INFO PER SERVING: Calories: 579, Fat: 53g, Net Carbs: 6g, Protein: 39g

Grilled Paprika Chicken with Steamed Broccoli

Ready in about: 17 minutes | Serves: 6

INGREDIENTS

Cooking spray
3 tbsp smoked paprika
Salt and black pepper to taste
2 tsp garlic powder

1 tbsp olive oil
6 chicken breasts
1 head broccoli, cut into florets

DIRECTIONS

Place broccoli florets onto the steamer basket over the boiling water; steam approximately 8 minutes or until crisp-tender. Set aside. Grease grill grate with cooking spray and preheat to 400ºF.

Combine paprika, salt, black pepper, and garlic powder in a bowl. Brush chicken with olive oil and sprinkle spice mixture over and massage with hands.

Grill chicken for 7 minutes per side until well-cooked, and plate. Serve warm with steamed broccoli.

NUTRITIONAL INFO PER SERVING: Calories 422, Fat 35.3g, Net Carbs 2g, Protein 26g

Sticky Cranberry Chicken Wings

Ready in about: 50 minutes | Serves: 6

INGREDIENTS

2 lb chicken wings
4 tbsp unsweetened cranberry puree
2 tbsp olive oil

Salt to taste
Sweet chili sauce to taste
Lemon juice from 1 lemon

DIRECTIONS

Preheat the oven (broiler side) to 400ºF. Then, in a bowl, mix the cranberry puree, olive oil, salt, sweet chili sauce, and lemon juice. After, add in the wings and toss to coat.

Place the chicken under the broiler, and cook for 45 minutes, turning once halfway.

Remove the chicken after and serve warm with a cranberry and cheese dipping sauce.

NUTRITIONAL INFO PER SERVING: Calories 152, Fat 8.5g, Net Carbs 1.6g, Protein 17.6g

Buttered Duck Breast

Ready in about: 30 minutes | Serves: 1

INGREDIENTS

1 medium duck breast, skin scored
1 tbsp heavy cream
2 tbsp butter

Salt and black pepper, to taste
1 cup kale
¼ tsp fresh sage

DIRECTIONS

Set the pan over medium-high heat and warm half of the butter. Place in sage and heavy cream, and cook for 2 minutes. Set another pan over medium-high heat. Place in the remaining butter and duck breast as the skin side faces down, cook for 4 minutes, flip, and cook for 3 more minutes.

Place the kale to the pan containing the sauce, cook for 1 minute. Set the duck breast on a flat surface and slice. Arrange the duck slices on a platter and drizzle over the sauce.

NUTRITIONAL INFO PER SERVING: Calories 547, Fat 46g, Net Carbs 2g, Protein 35g

Roasted Chicken with Tarragon

Ready in about: 50 minutes | Serves: 4

INGREDIENTS

2 lb chicken thighs
2 lb radishes, sliced
4 ¼ oz butter

1 tbsp tarragon
Salt and black pepper, to taste
1 cup mayonnaise

Set an oven to 400ºF and grease a baking dish. Add in the chicken, radishes, tarragon, pepper, and salt. Place in butter then set into the oven and cook for 40 minutes. Kill the heat, set on a serving plate and enjoy alongside mayonnaise.

NUTRITIONAL INFO PER SERVING: Calories: 415, Fat: 23g, Net Carbs: 5.5g, Protein: 42g

Lemon Chicken Bake

Ready in about: 55 minutes | Serves: 6

INGREDIENTS

6 skinless chicken breasts
1 parsnip, cut into wedges
Salt and ground black pepper, to taste

Juice from 2 lemons
Zest from 2 lemons
Lemon rinds from 2 lemons

DIRECTIONS

In a baking dish, add the chicken alongside pepper and salt. Sprinkle with lemon juice. Toss well to coat, place in parsnip, lemon rinds and lemon zest, set in an oven at 370ºF, and bake for 45 minutes.

Get rid of the lemon rinds, split the chicken onto plates, sprinkle sauce from the baking dish over.

NUTRITIONAL INFO PER SERVING: Calories 334, Fat 21g, Net Carbs 4.5g, Protein 25g

Spicy Chicken Kabobs

Ready in about: 1 hour and 20 minutes | Serves: 6

INGREDIENTS

2 pounds chicken breasts, cubed
2 tbsp olive oil
1 cup red bell pepper pieces

2 tbsp five spice powder
2 tbsp granulated sweetener
1 tbsp fish sauce

DIRECTIONS

Combine the sauces and seasonings in a bowl. Add the chicken, and let marinate for 1 hour in the fridge. Preheat the grill. Take 12 skewers and thread the chicken and bell peppers. Grill for 3 minutes per side.

NUTRITIONAL INFO PER SERVING: Calories 198, Fat: 13.5g, Net Carbs: 3.1g, Protein: 17.5g

Cheddar Chicken Tenders

Ready in about: 40 minutes | Serves: 4

INGREDIENTS

2 eggs
3 tbsp butter, melted
3 cups coarsely crushed cheddar cheese

½ cup pork rinds, crushed
1 lb chicken tenders
Pink salt to taste

DIRECTIONS

Preheat oven to 350ºF and line a baking sheet with parchment paper. Whisk the eggs with the butter in one bowl and mix the cheese and pork rinds in another bowl.

Season chicken with salt, dip in egg mixture, and coat generously in cheddar mixture. Place on baking sheet, cover with aluminium foil and bake for 25 minutes. Remove foil and bake further for 12 minutes to golden brown. Serve chicken with mustard dip.

NUTRITIONAL INFO PER SERVING: Calories 507, Fat 54g, Net Carbs 1.3g, Protein 42g

Turkey Burgers with Fried Brussels Sprouts

Ready in about: 30 minutes | Serves: 4

INGREDIENTS

For the chicken burgers

1 pound ground turkey
1 free-range egg
½ onion, chopped
1 tsp salt

½ tsp ground black pepper
1 tsp dried thyme
2 oz butter

For the fried Brussels sprouts

1 ½ lb Brussels sprouts, halved
3 oz butter

1 tsp salt
½ tsp ground black pepper

DIRECTIONS

Combine the burger ingredients in a mixing bowl. Create patties from the mixture. Set a large pan over medium-high heat, warm butter, and fry the patties until cooked completely.

Place on a plate and cover with aluminium foil to keep warm. Fry brussels sprouts in butter, season to your preference, then set to a bowl. Plate the burgers and brussels sprouts and serve.

NUTRITIONAL INFO PER SERVING: Calories: 443, Fat: 25g, Net Carbs: 5.8g, Protein: 31g

Pancetta & Chicken Casserole

Ready in about: 40 minutes | Serves: 3

INGREDIENTS

8 pancetta strips, chopped
¼ cup Dijon mustard
Salt and black pepper, to taste
1 onion, chopped

1 tbsp olive oil
1 ½ cups chicken stock
3 chicken breasts, skinless and boneless
¼ tsp sweet paprika

DIRECTIONS

Using a bowl, combine the pepper, salt, and mustard. Sprinkle this on chicken breasts and massage. Set a pan over medium-high heat, stir in the pancetta, cook until it browns, and remove to a plate. Place oil in the same pan and heat over medium-high heat, add in the chicken breasts, cook for each side for 2 minutes and set aside.

Place in the stock, and bring to a simmer. Stir in pepper, pancetta, salt, and onions. Return the chicken to the pan as well, stir gently, and simmer for 20 minutes over medium heat, turning the meat halfway through. Split the chicken on serving plates, sprinkle the sauce over it to serve.

NUTRITIONAL INFO PER SERVING: Calories 313, Fat 18g, Net Carbs 3g, Protein 26g

Chicken & Squash Traybake

Ready in about: 60 minutes | Serves: 4

INGREDIENTS

2 lb chicken thighs
1 pound butternut squash, cubed
½ cup black olives, pitted
¼ cup olive oil

5 garlic cloves, sliced
1 tbsp dried oregano
Salt and black pepper, to taste

DIRECTIONS

Set oven to 400ºF and grease a baking dish. Place in the chicken with the skin down. Set the garlic, olives and butternut squash around the chicken then drizzle with oil.

Spread pepper, salt, and thyme over the mixture then add into the oven. Cook for 45 minutes.

NUTRITIONAL INFO PER SERVING: Calories: 411, Fat: 15g, Net Carbs: 5.5g, Protein: 31g

Duck & Vegetable Casserole

Ready in about: 20 minutes | Serves: 2

INGREDIENTS

2 duck breasts, skin on and sliced
2 zucchinis, sliced
1 tbsp coconut oil
1 green onion bunch, chopped

1 carrot, chopped
2 green bell peppers, seeded and chopped
Salt and ground black pepper, to taste

DIRECTIONS

Set a pan over medium-high heat and warm oil, stir in the green onions, and cook for 2 minutes. Place in the zucchini, bell peppers, pepper, salt, and carrot, and cook for 10 minutes.

Set another pan over medium-high heat, add in duck slices and cook each side for 3 minutes. Pour the mixture into the vegetable pan. Cook for 3 minutes. Set in bowls and enjoy.

NUTRITIONAL INFO PER SERVING: Calories 433, Fat 21g, Net Carbs 8g, Protein 53g

Chicken with Acorn Squash & Goat's Cheesem

Ready in about: 1 hour 15 minutes | Serves: 6

INGREDIENTS

6 chicken breasts, skinless and boneless
1 lb acorn squash, peeled and sliced
Salt and ground black pepper, to taste

1 cup goat's cheese, shredded
Cooking spray

DIRECTIONS

Take cooking oil and spray on a baking dish, add in chicken breasts, pepper, squash, and salt and drizzle with olive. Transfer in the oven set at 420ºF, and bake for 1 hour. Scatter goat's cheese, and bake for 15 minutes. Remove to a serving plate and enjoy.

NUTRITIONAL INFO PER SERVING: Calories 235, Fat 16g, Net Carbs 5g, Protein 12g

Coconut Chicken Soup

Ready in about: 30 minutes | Serves: 4

INGREDIENTS

3 tbsp butter
4 ounces cream cheese
2 chicken breasts, diced
4 cups chicken stock

Salt and black pepper, to taste
½ cup coconut cream
¼ cup celery, chopped

DIRECTIONS

In the blender, combine stock, butter, coconut cream, salt, cream cheese, and pepper. Remove to a pot, heat over medium heat, and stir in the chicken and celery. Simmer for 15 minutes, separate into bowls, and enjoy.

NUTRITIONAL INFO PER SERVING: Calories 387, Fat 23g, Net Carbs 5g, Protein 31g

Chicken with Green Sauce

Ready in about: 35 minutes | Serves: 4

INGREDIENTS

2 tbsp butter
4 scallions, chopped
4 chicken breasts, skinless and boneless

Salt and black pepper, to taste
6 ounces sour cream
2 tbsp fresh dill, chopped

DIRECTIONS

Heat a pan with the butter over medium-high heat, add in the chicken, season with pepper and salt, and fry for 2-3 per side until golden. Transfer to a baking dish and cook in the oven for 15 minutes at 390ºF, until no longer pink.

To the pan add scallions, and cook for 2 minutes. Pour in the sour cream, warm through without boil. Slice the chicken and serve on a platter with green sauce spooned over.

NUTRITIONAL INFO PER SERVING: Calories 236, Fat 9g, Net Carbs 2.3g, Protein 18g

Chicken, Eggplant and Gruyere Gratin

Ready in about: 55 minutes | Serves: 4

INGREDIENTS

3 tbsp butter
1 eggplant, chopped
2 tbsp gruyere cheese, grated

Salt and black pepper, to taste
2 garlic cloves, minced
6 chicken thighs

DIRECTIONS

Set a pan over medium heat and warm 1 tablespoon butter, place in the chicken thighs, season with pepper and salt, cook each side for 3 minutes and lay them in a baking dish. In the same pan melt the rest of the butter and cook the garlic for 1 minute.

Stir in the eggplant, pepper, and salt, and cook for 10 minutes. Ladle this mixture over the chicken, spread with the cheese, set in the oven at 350ºF, and bake for 30 minutes. Turn on the oven's broiler, and broil everything for 2 minutes. Split among serving plates and enjoy.

NUTRITIONAL INFO PER SERVING: Calories 412, Fat 37g, Net Carbs 5g, Protein 34g

Chicken and Bacon Rolls

Ready in about: 45 minutes | Serves: 4

INGREDIENTS

1 tbsp fresh chives, chopped
8 ounces blue cheese
2 pounds chicken breasts, skinless,
boneless, halved

12 bacon slices
2 tomatoes, chopped
Salt and ground black pepper, to taste

DIRECTIONS

Set a pan over medium heat, place in the bacon, cook until halfway done, remove to paper towels, and drain the grease. Using a bowl, stir together the blue cheese, chives, tomatoes, pepper, and salt.

Use a meat tenderizer to flatten the chicken breasts well, season and lay the cream cheese mixture on top. Roll them up, and wrap each in a bacon slice. Place the wrapped chicken breasts in a greased baking dish, and roast in the oven at 370ºF for 30 minutes. Serve on top of wilted kale.

NUTRITIONAL INFO PER SERVING: Calories 623, Fat 48g, Net Carbs 5g, Protein 38g

Chicken Breasts with Walnut Crust

Ready in about: 30 minutes | Serves: 4

INGREDIENTS

1 egg, whisked
Salt and black pepper, to taste
3 tbsp coconut oil

1 ½ cups walnuts, ground
4 chicken breast halves, boneless and
skinless

DIRECTIONS

Using a bowl, add in walnuts and the whisked egg in another. Season the chicken, dip in the egg and then in pecans. Warm oil in a pan over medium-high heat and brown the chicken.

Remove the chicken pieces to a baking sheet, set in the oven, and bake for 10 minutes at 350º F. Serve topped with lemon slices.

NUTRITIONAL INFO PER SERVING: Calories 322, Fat 18g, Net Carbs 1.5g, Protein 35g

Fried Chicken Breasts

Ready in about: 20 minutes | Serves: 4

INGREDIENTS

2 chicken breasts, cut into strips
4 ounces pork rinds, crushed
2 cups coconut oil

16 ounces jarred pickle juice
2 eggs, whisked

DIRECTIONS

Using a bowl, combine the chicken breast pieces with pickle juice and refrigerate for 12 hours while covered. Set the eggs in a bowl, and pork rinds in a separate one. Dip the chicken pieces in the eggs, and then in pork rinds, and ensure they are well coated.

Set a pan over medium-high heat and warm oil, fry the chicken for 3 minutes on each side, remove to paper towels, drain the excess grease, and enjoy.

NUTRITIONAL INFO PER SERVING: Calories 387, Fat 16g, Net Carbs 2.5g, Protein 23g

Paprika Chicken with Cream Sauce

Ready in about: 50 minutes | Serves: 4

INGREDIENTS

1 pound chicken thighs
Salt and black pepper, to taste
1 tsp onion powder

¼ cup heavy cream
2 tbsp butter
2 tbsp sweet paprika

DIRECTIONS

Using a bowl, combine the paprika with onion powder, pepper, and salt. Season chicken pieces with this mixture and lay on a lined baking sheet; bake for 40 minutes in the oven at 400ºF. Split the chicken in serving plates, and set aside.

Add the cooking juices to a skillet over medium heat, and mix with the heavy cream and butter. Cook for 5-6 minutes until the sauce is thickened. Sprinkle the sauce over the chicken and serve.

NUTRITIONAL INFO PER SERVING: Calories 381, Fat 33g, Net Carbs 2.6g, Protein 31.3g

PORK, BEEF & LAMB RECIPES

Grilled Pork Loin Chops with Barbecue Sauce

Ready in about: 1 hour 47 minutes | Serves: 4

INGREDIENTS

4 (6 oz) thick-cut pork loin chops, boneless
½ cup sugar-free BBQ sauce
1 tsp black pepper

1 tbsp erythritol
½ tsp ginger powder
2 tsp sweet paprika

DIRECTIONS

In a bowl, mix the black pepper, erythritol, ginger powder, and sweet paprika, and rub the pork chops on all sides with the mixture. Then, cover the pork chops with plastic wraps and place it in the refrigerator to marinate for 1 hour 30 minutes.

Preheat the grill to 450ºF. Unwrap the meat, place on the grill grate, and cook for 2 minutes per side. Reduce the heat and brush the BBQ sauce on the meat, cover the lid, and grill them for 5 minutes.

Open the lid, turn the meat and brush again with barbecue sauce. Continue cooking covered for 5 minutes. Remove the meat to a serving platter and serve with steamed vegetables.

NUTRITIONAL INFO PER SERVING: Calories 363, Fat 26.6g, Net Carbs 0g, Protein 34.1g

Balsamic Grilled Pork Chops

Ready in about: 2 hours 20 minutes | Serves: 6

INGREDIENTS

6 pork loin chops, boneless
2 tbsp erythritol
¼ cup balsamic vinegar
3 cloves garlic, minced

¼ cup olive oil
¼ tsp salt
Black pepper to taste

DIRECTIONS

Put the pork in the plastic bag. In a bowl, mix the erythritol, balsamic vinegar, garlic, olive oil, salt, pepper, and pour the sauce over the pork. Seal the bag, shake it, and place in the refrigerator.

Marinate the pork for 1 to 2 hours. Preheat the grill on medium-high heat, remove the pork when ready, and grill covered for 10 to 12 minutes on each side. Remove the pork chops, let them sit for 4 minutes, and serve with a syrupy parsnip sauté.

NUTRITIONAL INFO PER SERVING: Calories 418, Fat 26.8g, Net Carbs 1.5g, Protein 38.1g

Charred Tenderloin with Lemon Chimichurri

Ready in about: 64 minutes | Serves: 4

INGREDIENTS

Lemon Chimichurri

1 lemon, juiced
¼ cup chopped mint leaves
¼ cup chopped oregano leaves

2 cloves garlic, minced
¼ cup olive oil
Salt to taste

Pork

1 (4 lb) pork tenderloin
Salt and black pepper to season

Olive oil for rubbing

DIRECTIONS

Make the lemon chimichurri to have the flavors incorporate while the pork cooks.

In a bowl, mix the mint, oregano, and garlic. Then, add the lemon juice, olive oil, and salt, and combine well. Set the sauce aside in room temperature.

Preheat the charcoal grill to 450ºF in medium-high heat creating a direct heat area and indirect heat area. Rub the pork with olive oil, season with salt and pepper. Place the meat over direct heat and sear for 3 minutes on each side, after which, move to the indirect heat area.

Close the lid and cook for 25 minutes on one side, then open, turn the meat, and grill closed for 20 minutes on the other side. Remove the pork from the grill and let it sit for 5 minutes before slicing. Spoon lemon chimichurri over the pork and serve with a fresh salad.

NUTRITIONAL INFO PER SERVING: Calories 388, Fat 18g, Net Carbs 2.1g, Protein 28g

Pork Nachos

Ready in about: 15 minutes | Serves: 4

INGREDIENTS

1 bag low carb tortilla chips
2 cups leftover pulled pork
1 red bell pepper, seeded and chopped

1 red onion, diced
2 cups shredded Monterey Jack cheese

DIRECTIONS

Preheat oven to 350ºF. Arrange the chips in a medium cast iron pan, scatter pork over, followed by red bell pepper, and onion, and sprinkle with cheese. Cook in the oven for 10 minutes until the cheese has melted. Allow cooling for 3 minutes and serve.

NUTRITIONAL INFO PER SERVING: Calories 452, Fat 25g, Net Carbs 9.3g, Protein 22g

BBQ Pork Pizza with Goat Cheese

Ready in about: 30 minutes | Serves: 4

INGREDIENTS

1 low carb pizza bread
Olive oil for brushing
1 cup grated manchego cheese

2 cups leftover pulled pork
½ cup sugar-free BBQ sauce
1 cup crumbled goat cheese

DIRECTIONS

Preheat oven to 400ºF and put pizza bread on a pizza pan. Brush with olive oil and sprinkle the manchego cheese all over. Mix the pork with BBQ sauce and spread on the cheese. Drop goat cheese on top and bake for 25 minutes until the cheese has melted and golden brown on top. Slice the pizza with a cutter and serve warm.

NUTRITIONAL INFO PER SERVING: Calories 344, Fat 24g, Net Carbs 6,5g, Protein 18g

Lemon Pork Chops with Buttered Brussels Sprouts

Ready in about: 27 minutes | Serves: 6

INGREDIENTS

3 tbsp lemon juice
3 cloves garlic, pureed
1 tbsp olive oil
6 pork loin chops

1 tbsp butter
1 lb brussels sprouts, trimmed and halved
2 tbsp white wine
Salt and black pepper to taste

DIRECTIONS

Preheat broiler to 400ºF and mix the lemon juice, garlic, salt, pepper, and oil in a bowl.

Brush the pork with the mixture, place in a baking sheet, and cook for 6 minutes on each side until browned. Share into 6 plates and make the side dish.

Melt butter in a small wok or pan and cook in brussels sprouts for 5 minutes until tender. Drizzle with white wine, sprinkle with salt and black pepper and cook for another 5 minutes.

Ladle brussels sprouts to the side of the chops and serve with a hot sauce.

NUTRITIONAL INFO PER SERVING: Calories 549, Fat 48g, Net Carbs 2g, Protein 26g

Peanut Butter Pork Stir-Fry

Ready in about: 23 minutes | Serves: 4

INGREDIENTS

1 ½ tbsp ghee
2 lb pork loin, cut into strips
Pink salt and chili pepper to taste
2 tsp ginger-garlic paste

¼ cup chicken broth
5 tbsp peanut butter
2 cups mixed stir-fry vegetables

DIRECTIONS

Melt the ghee in a wok and mix the pork with salt, chili pepper, and ginger-garlic paste. Pour the pork into the wok and cook for 6 minutes until no longer pink.

Mix the peanut butter with some broth to be smooth, add to the pork and stir; cook for 2 minutes. Pour in the remaining broth, cook for 4 minutes, and add the mixed veggies. Simmer for 5 minutes.

Adjust the taste with salt and black pepper, and spoon the stir-fry to a side of cilantro cauli rice.

NUTRITIONAL INFO PER SERVING: Calories 571, Fat 49g, Net Carbs 1g, Protein 22.5g

Sweet Chipotle Grilled Ribs

Ready in about: 32 minutes | Serves: 4

INGREDIENTS

2 tbsp erythritol
Pink salt and black pepper to taste
1 tbsp olive oil
3 tsp chipotle powder

1 tsp garlic powder
1 lb spare ribs
4 tbsp sugar-free BBQ sauce + extra for serving

DIRECTIONS

Mix the erythritol, salt, pepper, oil, chipotle, and garlic powder. Brush on the meaty sides of the ribs and wrap in foil. Sit for 30 minutes to marinate.

Preheat oven to 400ºF, place wrapped ribs on a baking sheet, and cook for 40 minutes to be cooked through. Remove ribs and aluminium foil, brush with BBQ sauce, and brown under the broiler for 10 minutes on both sides. Slice and serve with extra BBQ sauce and lettuce tomato salad.

NUTRITIONAL INFO PER SERVING: Calories 395, Fat 33g, Net Carbs 3g, Protein 21g

Zucchini Boats with Beef & Pimiento Rojo

Ready in about: 25 minutes | Serves: 4

INGREDIENTS

4 zucchinis
2 tbsp olive oil
1 ½ lb ground beef
1 medium red onion, chopped

2 tbsp chopped pimiento
Pink salt and black pepper to taste
1 cup grated yellow cheddar cheese

DIRECTIONS

Preheat oven to 350ºF.

Lay the zucchinis on a flat surface, trim off the ends and cut in half lengthwise. Scoop out pulp from each half with a spoon to make shells. Chop the pulp.

Heat oil in a skillet; add the ground beef, red onion, pimiento, and zucchini pulp, and season with salt and black pepper. Cook for 6 minutes while stirring to break up lumps until beef is no longer pink. Turn the heat off. Spoon the beef into the boats and sprinkle with cheddar cheese.

Place on a greased baking sheet and cook to melt the cheese for 15 minutes until zucchini boats are tender. Take out, cool for 2 minutes, and serve warm with a mixed green salad.

NUTRITIONAL INFO PER SERVING: Calories 335, Fat 24g, Net Carbs 7g, Protein 18g

Beef Cauliflower Curry

Ready in about: 26 minutes | Serves: 6

INGREDIENTS

1 tbsp olive oil
1 ½ lb ground beef
1 tbsp ginger-garlic paste
1 tsp garam masala

1 (7 oz) can whole tomatoes
1 head cauliflower, cut into florets
Pink salt and chili pepper to taste
¼ cup water

DIRECTIONS

Heat oil in a saucepan over medium heat, add the beef, ginger-garlic paste and season with garam masala. Cook for 5 minutes while breaking any lumps.

Stir in the tomatoes and cauliflower, season with salt and chili pepper, and cook covered for 6 minutes. Add the water and bring to a boil over medium heat for 10 minutes or until the water has reduced by half. Adjust taste with salt.

Spoon the curry into serving bowls and serve with shirataki rice.

NUTRITIONAL INFO PER SERVING: Calories 374, Fat 33g, Net Carbs 2g, Protein 22g

Spicy Spinach Pinwheel Steaks

Ready in about: 42 minutes | Serves: 6

INGREDIENTS

Cooking spray
1 ½ lb flank steak
Pink salt and black pepper to season
1 cup crumbled feta cheese

½ loose cup baby spinach
1 jalapeño, chopped
¼ cup chopped basil leaves

DIRECTIONS

Preheat oven to 400ºF and grease a baking sheet with cooking spray.

Wrap the steak in plastic wrap, place on a flat surface, and gently run a rolling pin over to flatten. Take off the wraps. Sprinkle with half of the feta cheese, top with spinach, jalapeno, basil leaves, and the remaining cheese. Roll the steak over on the stuffing and secure with toothpicks.

Place in the greased baking sheet and cook for 30 minutes, flipping once until nicely browned on the outside and the cheese melted within. Cool for 3 minutes, slice into pinwheels and serve with thyme sautéed mixed veggies.

NUTRITIONAL INFO PER SERVING: Calories 490, Fat 41g, Net Carbs 2g, Protein 28g

Herb Pork Chops with Raspberry Sauce

Ready in about: 17 minutes | Serves: 4

INGREDIENTS

1 tbsp olive oil + extra for brushing
2 lb pork chops
Pink salt and black pepper to taste
2 cups raspberries

¼ cup water
1 ½ tbsp Italian Herb mix
3 tbsp balsamic vinegar
2 tsp sugar-free Worcestershire sauce

DIRECTIONS

Heat oil in a skillet over medium heat, season the pork with salt and black pepper and cook for 5 minutes on each side. Put on serving plates and reserve the pork drippings.

Mash the raspberries with a fork in a bowl until jam-like. Pour into a saucepan, add the water, and herb mix. Bring to boil on low heat for 4 minutes. Stir in pork drippings, vinegar, and Worcestershire sauce. Simmer for 1 minute. Spoon sauce over the pork chops and serve with braised rapini.

NUTRITIONAL INFO PER SERVING: Calories 413, Fat 32.5g, Net Carbs 1.1g, Protein 26.3g

White Wine Lamb Chops

Ready in about: 1 hour and 25 minutes | Serves: 6

INGREDIENTS

6 lamb chops
1 tsp thyme
1 onion, sliced
3 garlic cloves, minced

2 tbsp olive oil
½ cup white wine
Salt and black pepper, to taste

DIRECTIONS

Heat the olive oil in a pan. Add onion and garlic and cook for 3 minutes, until soft. Rub the thyme over the lamb chops. Cook the lamb for about 3 minutes per side. Set aside.

Pour the white wine and 1 cup of water into the pan, bring the mixture to a boil. Cook until the liquid is reduced by half. Add the chops in the pan, reduce the heat, and let simmer for 1 hour.

NUTRITIONAL INFO PER SERVING: Calories 397, Fat: 30g, Net Carbs: 4.3g, Protein: 16g

Beef Tripe in Vegetable Sauté

Ready in about: 27 minutes + cooling time | Serves: 6

INGREDIENTS

1 ½ lb beef tripe
4 cups buttermilk
Pink salt to taste
2 tsp creole seasoning

3 tbsp olive oil
2 large onions, sliced
3 tomatoes, diced

DIRECTIONS

Put tripe in a bowl and cover with buttermilk. Refrigerate for 3 hours to extract bitterness and gamey taste. Remove from buttermilk, pat dry with paper towel, and season with salt and creole.

Heat 2 tablespoons of oil in a skillet over medium heat and brown the tripe on both sides for 6 minutes in total. Remove and set aside.

Add the remaining oil and sauté the onions for 3 minutes until soft. Include the tomatoes and cook for 10 minutes. Pour in a few tablespoons of water if necessary. Put the tripe in the sauce and cook for 3 minutes. Adjust taste with salt and serve with low carb rice.

NUTRITIONAL INFO PER SERVING: Calories 342, Fat 27g, Net Carbs 1g, Protein 22g

Beef Cotija Cheeseburger

Ready in about: 15 minutes | Serves: 4

INGREDIENTS

1 lb ground beef
1 tsp dried parsley
½ tsp sugar-free Worcestershire sauce

Salt and black pepper to taste
1 cup cotija cheese, shredded
4 low carb buns, halved

DIRECTIONS

Preheat a grill to 400ºF and grease the grate with cooking spray.

Mix the beef, parsley, Worcestershire sauce, salt, and black pepper with your hands until evenly combined. Make medium sized patties out of the mixture, about 4 patties. Cook on the grill for 7 minutes one side to be cooked through and no longer pink.

Flip the patties and top with cheese. Cook for another 7 minutes to be well done while the cheese melts onto the meat. Remove the patties and sandwich into two halves of a bun each. Serve with a tomato dipping sauce and zucchini fries.

NUTRITIONAL INFO PER SERVING: Calories 386, Fat 32g, Net Carbs 2g, Protein 21g

Bacon Smothered Pork Chops

Ready in about: 25 minutes | Serves: 6

INGREDIENTS

7 strips bacon, chopped
6 pork chops
Pink salt and black pepper to taste

5 sprigs fresh thyme + extra to garnish
¼ cup chicken broth
½ cup heavy cream

DIRECTIONS

Cook bacon in a large skillet on medium heat for 5 minutes to be crispy. Remove with a slotted spoon onto a paper towel-lined plate to soak up excess fat.

Season pork chops with salt and black pepper and brown in the bacon fat for 4 minutes on each side. Remove to the bacon plate. Stir in the thyme, chicken broth, and heavy cream and simmer for 5 minutes. Season with salt and black pepper.

Return the chops and bacon, and cook further for another 2 minutes. Serve chops and a generous ladle of sauce with cauli mash. Garnish with thyme leaves.

NUTRITIONAL INFO PER SERVING: Calories 435, Fat 37g, Net Carbs 3g, Protein 22g

Mustardy Pork Chops

Ready in about: 15 minutes | Serves: 4

INGREDIENTS

4 pork loin chops
1 tsp Dijon mustard
1 tbsp soy sauce
1 tsp lemon juice

1 tbsp water
Salt and black pepper, to taste
1 tbsp butter
A bunch of scallions, chopped

DIRECTIONS

Using a bowl, combine the water with lemon juice, mustard and soy sauce. Set a pan over medium heat and warm butter, add in the pork chops, season with lemon pepper, salt, and pepper, cook for 4 minutes, turn, and cook for additional 4 minutes. Remove the pork chops to a plate and keep warm.

In the same pan , pour in the mustard sauce, and simmer for 5 minutes. Spread this over pork, top with scallions, and enjoy.

NUTRITIONAL INFO PER SERVING: Calories 382, Fat 21.5g, Net Carbs 1.2g, Protein 38g

Beef Skewers with Ranch Dressing

Ready in about: 25 minutes | Serves: 4

INGREDIENTS

1 lb sirloin steak, boneless, cubed
¼ cup ranch dressing, divided

Chopped scallions to garnish

DIRECTIONS

Preheat the grill on medium heat to 400ºF and thread the beef cubes on the skewers, about 4 to 5 cubes per skewer. Brush half of the ranch dressing on the skewers (all around) and place them on the grill grate to cook for 6 minutes. Turn the skewers once and cook further for 6 minutes.

Brush the remaining ranch dressing on the meat and cook them for 1 more minute on each side. Plate, garnish with the scallions, and serve with a mixed veggie salad, and extra ranch dressing.

NUTRITIONAL INFO PER SERVING: Calories 230, Fat 14g, Net Carbs 3g, Protein 21g

Lamb Shashlyk

Ready in about: 20 minutes | Serves: 4

INGREDIENTS

1 pound ground lamb
¼ tsp cinnamon
1 egg

1 grated onion
Salt and ground pepper, to taste

DIRECTIONS

Place all ingredients in a bowl. Mix with your hands to combine well. Divide the meat into 4 pieces. Shape all meat portions around previously-soaked skewers. Preheat your grill to medium. Grill the kebabs for about 5 minutes per side.

NUTRITIONAL INFO PER SERVING: Calories 467, Fat: 37g, Net Carbs: 3.2g, Protein: 27g

Adobo Beef Fajitas

Ready in about: 7 minutes | Serves: 4

INGREDIENTS

2 lb skirt steak, cut in halves
2 tbsp Adobo seasoning
Pink salt to taste
2 tbsp olive oil

2 large white onion, chopped
1 cup sliced mixed bell peppers, chopped
12 low carb tortillas

DIRECTIONS

Season the steak with adobo and marinate in the fridge for one hour.

Preheat grill to 425ºF and cook steak for 6 minutes on each side, flipping once until lightly browned. Remove from heat and wrap in foil and let sit for 10 minutes. This allows the meat to cook in its heat for a few more minutes before slicing.

Heat the olive oil in a skillet over medium heat and sauté the onion and bell peppers for 5 minutes or until soft. Cut steak against the grain into strips and share on the tortillas. Top with vegetables and serve with guacamole.

NUTRITIONAL INFO PER SERVING: Calories 348, Fat 25g, Net Carbs 5g, Protein 18g

Ribeye Steak with Shitake Mushrooms

Ready in about: 25 minutes | Serves: 1

INGREDIENTS

6 ounces ribeye steak
2 tbsp butter
1 tsp olive oil

½ cup shitake mushrooms, sliced
Salt and ground pepper, to taste

DIRECTIONS

Heat the olive oil in a pan over medium heat. Rub the steak with salt and pepper and cook about 4 minutes per side; set aside. Melt the butter in the pan and cook the shitakes for 4 minutes. Pour the butter and mushrooms over the steak to serve.

NUTRITIONAL INFO PER SERVING: Calories 478, Fat: 31g, Net Carbs: 3g, Protein: 33g

Beef and Egg Rice Bowls

Ready in about: 22 minutes | Serves: 4

INGREDIENTS

2 cups cauli rice
3 cups frozen mixed vegetables
3 tbsp ghee
1 lb skirt steak

Salt and black pepper to taste
4 fresh eggs
Hot sauce (sugar-free) for topping

DIRECTIONS

Mix the cauli rice and mixed vegetables in a bowl, sprinkle with a little water, and steam in the microwave for 1 minute to be tender. Share into 4 serving bowls.

Melt the ghee in a skillet, season the beef with salt and pepper, and brown for 5 minutes on each side. Use a perforated spoon to ladle the meat onto the vegetables.

Wipe out the skillet and return to medium heat, crack in an egg, season with salt and pepper and cook until the egg white has set, but the yolk is still runny 3 minutes. Remove egg onto the vegetable bowl and fry the remaining 3 eggs. Add to the other bowls.

Drizzle the beef bowls with hot sauce and serve.

NUTRITIONAL INFO PER SERVING: Calories 320, Fat 26g, Net Carbs 4g, Protein 15g

Beef Cheeseburger Casserole

Ready in about: 30 minutes | Serves: 6

INGREDIENTS

2 lb ground beef
Pink salt and black pepper to taste
1 cup cauli rice
2 cups chopped cabbage

14 oz can diced tomatoes
¼ cup water
1 cup shredded colby jack cheese

DIRECTIONS

Preheat oven to 370ºF and grease a baking dish with cooking spray. Put beef in a pot and season with salt and black pepper and cook over medium heat for 6 minutes until no longer pink. Drain grease. Add cauli rice, cabbage, tomatoes, and water. Stir and bring to boil covered for 5 minutes to thicken the sauce. Adjust taste with salt and black pepper.

Spoon the beef mixture into the baking dish and spread evenly in the dish. Sprinkle with cheese and bake in the oven for 15 minutes until cheese has melted and golden brown. Remove and cool for 4 minutes and serve with low carb crusted bread.

NUTRITIONAL INFO PER SERVING: Calories 385, Fat 25g, Net Carbs 5g, Protein 20g

Rolled Shoulder with Basil and Pine Nuts

Ready in about: 1 hour 4 minutes | Serves: 4

INGREDIENTS

1 lb rolled lamb shoulder, boneless
1 ½ cups basil leaves, chopped
5 tbsp pine nuts, chopped

½ cup green olives, pitted and chopped
3 cloves garlic, minced
Salt and black pepper to taste

DIRECTIONS

Preheat the oven to 450ºF. In a bowl, combine the basil, pine nuts, olives, and garlic. Season with salt and black pepper.

Untie the lamb flat onto a chopping board, spread the basil mixture all over, and rub the spice into the meat. Roll the lamb over the spice mixture and tie it together using 3 to 4 strings of butcher's twine. Place the lamb onto a baking dish and cook in the oven for 10 minutes. Reduce the heat to 350ºF and continue cooking for 40 minutes.

When ready, transfer the meat to a cleaned chopping board; let it rest for 10 minutes before slicing. Serve with a side of equally roasted capsicums and root vegetables.

NUTRITIONAL INFO PER SERVING: Calories 547, Fat 37.7g, Net Carbs 2.2g, Protein 42.7g

Juicy Pork Medallions

Ready in about: 55 minutes | Serves: 4

INGREDIENTS

2 onions, chopped
6 bacon slices, chopped
½ cup vegetable stock

Salt and black pepper, to taste
1 pound pork tenderloin, cut into medallions

DIRECTIONS

Set a pan over medium heat, stir in the bacon, cook until crispy, and remove to a plate. Add onions, some pepper, and salt, and cook for 5 minutes; set to the same plate with bacon.

Add the pork medallions to the pan, season with pepper and salt, brown for 3 minutes on each side, turn, reduce heat to medium, and cook for 7 minutes. Stir in the stock, and cook for 2 minutes. Return the bacon and onions to the pan and cook for 1 minute.

NUTRITIONAL INFO PER SERVING: Calories 325, Fat 18g, Net Carbs 6g, Protein 36g

Jamaican Pork Oven Roast

Ready in about: 4 hours and 20 minutes | Serves: 12

INGREDIENTS

4 pounds pork roast
1 tbsp olive oil
¼ cup jerk spice blend

½ cup vegetable stock
Salt and ground pepper, to taste

DIRECTIONS

Rub the pork with olive oil and the spice blend. Heat a dutch oven over medium heat and sear the meat well on all sides. Add the broth. Cover the pot, reduce the heat, and let cook for 4 hours.

NUTRITIONAL INFO PER SERVING: Calories 282, Fat: 24g, Net Carbs: 0g, Protein: 23g

Greek Pork with Olives

Ready in about: 45 minutes | Serves: 4

INGREDIENTS

4 pork chops, bone-in
Salt and ground black pepper, to taste
1 tsp dried rosemary
3 garlic cloves, peeled and minced

½ cup kalamata olives, pitted and sliced
2 tbsp olive oil
¼ cup vegetable broth

Season pork chops with pepper and salt, and add in a roasting pan. Stir in the garlic, olives, olive oil, broth, and rosemary, set in the oven at 425ºF, and bake for 10 minutes. Reduce heat to 350ºF and roast for 25 minutes. Slice the pork, split among plates, and sprinkle with pan juices all over.

NUTRITIONAL INFO PER SERVING: Calories 415, Fat 25.2g, Net Carbs 2.2g, Protein 36g

Pulled Pork with Avocado

Ready in about: 55 minutes | Serves: 12

INGREDIENTS

4 pounds pork shoulder
1 tbsp avocado oil
½ cup beef stock

¼ cup jerk seasoning
6 avocado, sliced

DIRECTIONS

Rub the pork shoulder with jerk seasoning, and set in a greased baking dish. Pour in the stock, and cook for 1 hour 45 minutes in your oven at 350ºF covered with aluminium foil.

Discard the foil and cook for another 20 minutes. Leave to rest for 30 minutes, and shred it with 2 forks. Serve topped with avocado slices.

NUTRITIONAL INFO PER SERVING: Calories 567, Fat 42.6g, Net Carbs 4.1g, Protein 42g

Pork and Mushroom Bake

Ready in about: 1 hour and 15 minutes | Serves: 6

INGREDIENTS

1 onion, chopped
2 (10.5 oz) cans mushroom soup
6 pork chops

½ cup sliced mushrooms
Salt and ground pepper, to taste

DIRECTIONS

Preheat the oven to 370ºF.

Season the pork chops with salt and pepper, and place in a baking dish. Combine the mushroom soup, mushrooms, and onion, in a bowl. Pour this mixture over the pork chops. Bake for 45 minutes.

NUTRITIONAL INFO PER SERVING: Calories 403, Fat: 32.6g, Net Carbs: 8g, Protein: 19.4g

Beef Provençal

Ready in about: 50 minutes | Serves: 4

INGREDIENTS

12 ounces beef steak racks
2 fennel bulbs, sliced
Salt and black pepper, to taste
3 tbsp olive oil

½ cup apple cider vinegar
1 tsp herbs de Provence
1 tbsp swerve

DIRECTIONS

In a bowl, mix the fennel with 2 tbsp of oil, swerve, and vinegar, toss to coat well, and set to a baking dish. Season with herbs de Provence, pepper and salt, and cook in the oven at 400ºF for 15 minutes.

Sprinkle pepper and salt to the beef, place into an oiled pan over medium-high heat, and cook for a couple of minutes. Place the beef to the baking dish with the fennel, and bake for 20 minutes. Split everything among plates and enjoy.

NUTRITIONAL INFO PER SERVING: Calories 230, Fat 11.3g, Net Carbs 5.2g, Protein 19g

Paprika Pork Chops

Ready in about: 25 minutes | Serves: 4

INGREDIENTS

4 pork chops
Salt and black pepper, to taste
3 tbsp paprika

¾ cup cumin powder
1 tsp chili powder

DIRECTIONS

Using a bowl, combine the paprika with pepper, cumin, salt, and chili. Place in the pork chops and rub them well. Heat a grill over medium temperature, add in the pork chops, cook for 5 minutes, flip, and cook for 5 minutes. Serve with steamed veggies.

NUTRITIONAL INFO PER SERVING: Calories 349, Fat 18.5g, Net Carbs 4g, Protein 41.8g

SEAFOOD & FISH RECIPES

Red Cabbage Tilapia Taco Bowl

Ready in about: 17 minutes | Serves: 4

INGREDIENTS

2 cups cauli rice
Water for sprinkling
2 tsp ghee
4 tilapia fillets, cut into cubes

¼ tsp taco seasoning
Pink salt and chili pepper to taste
¼ head red cabbage, shredded
1 ripe avocado, pitted and chopped

DIRECTIONS

Sprinkle cauli rice in a bowl with a little water and microwave for 3 minutes. Fluff after with a fork and set aside. Melt ghee in a skillet over medium heat, rub the tilapia with the taco seasoning, salt, and chili pepper, and fry until brown on all sides, for about 8 minutes in total.

Transfer to a plate and set aside. In 4 serving bowls, share the cauli rice, cabbage, fish, and avocado. Serve with chipotle lime sour cream dressing.

NUTRITIONAL INFO PER SERVING: Calories 269, Fat 23.4g, Net Carbs 4g, Protein 16.5g

Sour Cream Salmon with Parmesan

Ready in about: 25 minutes | Serves: 4

INGREDIENTS

1 cup sour cream
½ tbsp minced dill
½ lemon, zested and juiced

Pink salt and black pepper to season
4 salmon steaks
½ cup grated Parmesan cheese

DIRECTIONS

Preheat oven to 400ºF and line a baking sheet with parchment paper; set aside. In a bowl, mix the sour cream, dill, lemon zest, Juice, salt, and pepper, and set aside.

Season the fish with salt and black pepper, drizzle lemon juice on both sides of the fish and arrange them in the baking sheet. Spread the sour cream mixture on each fish and sprinkle with Parmesan.

Bake fish for 15 minutes and after broil the top for 2 minutes with a close watch for a nice a brown color. Plate the fish and serve with buttery green beans.

NUTRITIONAL INFO PER SERVING: Calories 288, Fat 23.4g, Net Carbs 1.2g, Protein 16.2g

Spicy Sea Bass with Hazelnuts

Ready in about: 30 minutes | Serves: 2

INGREDIENTS

2 sea bass fillets
2 tbsp butter

¼ cup roasted hazelnuts
A pinch of cayenne pepper

DIRECTIONS

Preheat your oven to 425 ºF. Line a baking dish with waxed paper. Melt the butter and brush it over the fish. In a food processor, combine the rest of the ingredients. Coat the sea bass with the hazelnut mixture. Place in the oven and bake for about 15 minutes.

NUTRITIONAL INFO PER SERVING: Calories 467, Fat: 31g, Net Carbs: 2.8g, Protein: 40g

Sushi Shrimp Rolls

Ready in about: 10 minutes | Serves: 5

INGREDIENTS

2 cups cooked and chopped shrimp
1 tbsp sriracha sauce
¼ cucumber, julienned

5 hand roll nori sheets
¼ cup mayonnaise

DIRECTIONS

Combine shrimp, mayonnaise, and sriracha in a bowl. Lay out a single nori sheet on a flat surface and spread about 1/5 of the shrimp mixture. Roll the nori sheet as desired. Repeat with the other ingredients.

NUTRITIONAL INFO PER SERVING: Calories 216, Fat: 10g, Net Carbs: 1g, Protein: 18.7g

Coconut Crab Patties

Ready in about: 15 minutes | Serves: 8

INGREDIENTS

2 tbsp coconut oil
1 tbsp lemon juice
1 cup lump crab meat

2 tsp Dijon mustard
1 egg, beaten
1 ½ tbsp coconut flour

DIRECTIONS

In a bowl to the crabmeat add all the ingredients, except for coconut oil; mix well to combine. Make patties out of the mixture. Melt the coconut oil in a skillet over medium heat. Add the crab patties and cook for about 2-3 minutes per side.

NUTRITIONAL INFO PER SERVING: Calories 215, Fat: 11.5g, Net Carbs: 3.6g, Protein: 15.3g

Lemon Garlic Shrimp

Ready in about: 22 minutes | Serves: 6

INGREDIENTS

½ cup butter, divided
2 lb shrimp, peeled and deveined
Pink salt and black pepper to taste
¼ tsp sweet paprika

1 tbsp minced garlic
3 tbsp water
1 lemon, zested and juiced
2 tbsp chopped parsley

DIRECTIONS

Melt half of the butter in a large skillet over medium heat, season the shrimp with salt, pepper, paprika, and add to the butter. Stir in the garlic and cook the shrimp for 4 minutes on both sides until pink. Remove into a bowl and set aside.

Put the remaining butter in the skillet; include the lemon zest, juice, and water. Cook until the butter has melted about 1 minute. Add the shrimp, parsley, and adjust taste with salt and black pepper. Cook for 2 minutes on low heat. Serve the shrimp and sauce with squash pasta.

NUTRITIONAL INFO PER SERVING: Calories 258, Fat 22g, Net Carbs 2g, Protein 13g

Seared Scallops with Chorizo & Asiago Cheese

Ready in about: 15 minutes | Serves: 4

INGREDIENTS

2 tbsp ghee
16 fresh scallops
8 ounces chorizo, chopped
1 red bell pepper, seeds removed, sliced

1 cup red onions, finely chopped
1 cup asiago cheese, grated
Salt and black pepper to taste

DIRECTIONS

Melt half of the ghee in a skillet over medium heat, and cook the onion and bell pepper for 5 minutes until tender. Add the chorizo and stir-fry for another 3 minutes. Remove and set aside.

Pat dry the scallops with paper towels, and season with salt and pepper. Add the remaining ghee to the skillet and sear the scallops for 2 minutes on each side to have a golden brown color. Add the chorizo mixture back and warm through. Transfer to serving platter and top with asiago cheese.

NUTRITIONAL INFO PER SERVING: Calories 491, Fat 32g, Net Carbs 5g, Protein 36g

Cod in Garlic Butter Sauce

Ready in about: 20 minutes | Serves: 6

INGREDIENTS

2 tsp olive oil
6 Alaska cod fillets
Salt and black pepper to taste
4 tbsp salted butter

4 cloves garlic, minced
¼ cup lemon juice
3 tbsp white wine
2 tbsp chopped chives

DIRECTIONS

Heat the oil in a skillet over medium heat and season the cod with salt and black pepper. Fry the fillets in the oil for 4 minutes on one side, flip and cook for 1 minute. Take out, plate, and set aside.

In another skillet over low heat, melt the butter and sauté the garlic for 3 minutes. Add the lemon juice, wine, and chives. Season with salt, black pepper, and cook for 3 minutes until the wine slightly reduces. Put the fish in the skillet, spoon sauce over, cook for 30 seconds and turn the heat off.

Divide fish into 6 plates, top with sauce, and serve with buttered green beans.

NUTRITIONAL INFO PER SERVING: Calories 264, Fat 17.3g, Net Carbs 2.3g, Protein 20g

Parmesan Fish Bake

Ready in about: 40 minutes | Serves: 4

INGREDIENTS

Cooking spray
2 salmon fillets, cubed
3 white fish, cubed
1 broccoli, cut into florets
1 tbsp butter, melted

Pink salt and black pepper to taste
1 cup crème fraiche
¼ cup grated Parmesan cheese
Grated Parmesan cheese for topping

DIRECTIONS

Preheat oven to 400ºF and grease an 8 x 8-casserole dish with cooking spray. Toss the fish cubes and broccoli in butter and season with salt and black pepper to taste. Spread in the greased dish.

Mix the crème fraiche with parmesan cheese, pour and smear the cream on the fish, and sprinkle with some more parmesan. Bake for 25 to 30 minutes until golden brown on top, take the dish out, sit for 5 minutes and spoon into plates. Serve with lemon-mustard asparagus.

NUTRITIONAL INFO PER SERVING: Calories 354, Fat 17g, Net Carbs 4g, Protein 28g

Smoked Mackerel Patties

Ready in about: 30 minutes | Serves: 6

INGREDIENTS

1 turnip, peeled and diced
1 ½ cups water
Pink salt and chili pepper to taste
3 tbsp olive oil + for rubbing
4 smoked mackerel steaks, bones removed,

flaked
3 eggs, beaten
2 tbsp mayonnaise
1 tbsp pork rinds, crushed

DIRECTIONS

Bring the turnip to boil in salted water in a saucepan over medium heat for 8 minutes or until tender. Drain the turnip through a colander, transfer to a mixing bowl, and mash the lumps.

Add the mackerel, eggs, mayonnaise, pork rinds, salt, and chili pepper. With gloves on your hands, mix and make 6 compact patties.

Heat olive oil in a skillet over medium heat and fry the patties for 3 minutes on each side to be golden brown. Remove onto a wire rack to cool. Serve cakes with sesame lime dipping sauce.

NUTRITIONAL INFO PER SERVING: Calories 324, Fat 27.1g, Net Carbs 2.2g, Protein 16g

MEATLESS MEALS

Cauliflower Gouda Casserole

Ready in about: 21 minutes | Serves: 4

INGREDIENTS

2 heads cauliflower, cut into florets
¼ cup butter, cubed
2 tbsp melted butter
1 white onion, chopped
Pink salt and black pepper to taste

¼ almond milk
½ cup almond flour
1 ½ cups grated gouda cheese
Water for sprinkling

DIRECTIONS

Preheat oven to 350ºF and put the cauli florets in a large microwave-safe bowl. Sprinkle with water, and steam in the microwave for 4 to 5 minutes.

Melt the ¼ cup of butter in a saucepan over medium heat and sauté the onions for 3 minutes. Add the cauliflower, season with salt and black pepper and mix in almond milk. Simmer for 3 minutes.

Mix the remaining melted butter with almond flour. Stir into the cauliflower as well as half of the cheese. Sprinkle the top with the remaining cheese and bake for 10 minutes until the cheese has melted and golden brown on the top. Plate the bake and serve with arugula salad.

NUTRITIONAL INFO PER SERVING: Calories 215, Fat 15g, Net Carbs 4g, Protein 12g

Zucchini Lasagna with Ricotta and Spinach

Ready in about: 50 minutes | Serves: 4

INGREDIENTS

Cooking spray
2 zucchinis, sliced
Salt and black pepper to taste
2 cups ricotta cheese

2 cups shredded mozzarella cheese
3 cups tomato sauce
1 cup packed baby spinach

DIRECTIONS

Preheat oven to 370ºF and grease a baking dish with cooking spray.

Put the zucchini slices in a colander and sprinkle with salt. Let sit and drain liquid for 5 minutes and pat dry with paper towels. Mix the ricotta, mozzarella, salt, and pepper to evenly combine and spread ¼ cup of the mixture in the bottom of the baking dish.

Layer a third of the zucchini slices on top spread 1 cup of tomato sauce over, and scatter one-third cup of spinach on top. Repeat the layering process two more times to exhaust the ingredients while making sure to layer with the last ¼ cup of cheese mixture finally.

Grease one end of foil with cooking spray and cover the baking dish with the foil. Bake for 35 minutes, remove foil, and bake further for 5 to 10 minutes or until the cheese has a nice golden brown color. Remove the dish, sit for 5 minutes, make slices of the lasagna, and serve warm.

NUTRITIONAL INFO PER SERVING: Calories 390, Fat 39g, Net Carbs 2g, Protein 7g

Vegetable Tempeh Kabobs

Ready in about: 2 hours 26 minutes | Serves: 4

INGREDIENTS

10 oz tempeh, cut into chunks
1 ½ cups water
1 red onion, cut into chunks
1 red bell pepper, cut chunks

1 yellow bell pepper, cut into chunks
2 tbsp olive oil
1 cup sugar-free barbecue sauce

DIRECTIONS

Bring the water to boil in a pot over medium heat and once it has boiled, turn the heat off, and add the tempeh. Cover the pot and let the tempeh steam for 5 minutes to remove its bitterness.

Drain the tempeh after. Pour the barbecue sauce in a bowl, add the tempeh to it, and coat with the sauce. Cover the bowl and marinate in the fridge for 2 hours.

Preheat a grill to 350ºF, and thread the tempeh, yellow bell pepper, red bell pepper, and onion.

Brush the grate of the grill with olive oil, place the skewers on it, and brush with barbecue sauce. Cook the kabobs for 3 minutes on each side while rotating and brushing with more barbecue sauce.

Once ready, transfer the kabobs to a plate and serve with lemon cauli couscous and a tomato sauce.

NUTRITIONAL INFO PER SERVING: Calories 228, Fat 15g, Net Carbs 3.6g, Protein 13.2g

Creamy Vegetable Stew

Ready in about: 32 minutes | Serves: 4

INGREDIENTS

2 tbsp ghee
1 tbsp onion garlic puree
4 medium carrots, peeled and chopped
1 large head cauliflower, cut into florets

2 cups green beans, halved
Salt and black pepper to taste
1 cup water
1 ½ cups heavy cream

DIRECTIONS

Melt ghee in a saucepan over medium heat and sauté onion-garlic puree to be fragrant, 2 minutes.

Stir in carrots, cauliflower, and green beans, salt, and pepper, add the water, stir again, and cook the vegetables on low heat for 25 minutes to soften. Mix in the heavy cream to be incorporated, turn the heat off, and adjust the taste with salt and pepper. Serve the stew with almond flour bread.

NUTRITIONAL INFO PER SERVING: Calories 310, Fat 26.4g, Net Carbs 6g, Protein 8g

Parmesan Roasted Cabbage

Ready in about: 25 minutes | Serves: 4

INGREDIENTS

Cooking spray
1 large head green cabbage
4 tbsp melted butter
1 tsp garlic powder

Salt and black pepper to taste
1 cup grated Parmesan cheese
Grated Parmesan cheese for topping
1 tbsp chopped parsley to garnish

DIRECTIONS

Preheat oven to 400ºF, line a baking sheet with foil, and grease with cooking spray.

Stand the cabbage and run a knife from the top to bottom to cut the cabbage into wedges. Remove stems and wilted leaves. Mix the butter, garlic, salt, and black pepper until evenly combined.

Brush the mixture on all sides of the cabbage wedges and sprinkle with parmesan cheese.

Place on the baking sheet, and bake for 20 minutes to soften the cabbage and melt the cheese. Remove the cabbages when golden brown, plate and sprinkle with extra cheese and parsley. Serve warm with pan-glazed tofu.

NUTRITIONAL INFO PER SERVING: Calories 268, Fat 19.3g, Net Carbs 4g, Protein 17.5g

Parsnip Chips with Avocado Dip

Ready in about: 20 minutes | Serves: 6

INGREDIENTS

2 avocados, pitted
2 tsp lime juice
Salt and black pepper, to taste

2 garlic cloves, minced
2 tbsp olive oil

For Parsnip Chips

3 cups parsnips, sliced
1 tbsp olive oil

Sea salt and garlic powder, to taste

DIRECTIONS

Use a fork to mash avocado pulp. Stir in fresh lime juice, pepper, 2 tbsp of olive oil, garlic, and salt until well combined. Remove to a bowl and set the oven to 300 ºF. Grease a baking sheet with spray.

Set parsnip slices on the baking sheet; toss with garlic powder, 1 tbps of olive oil, and salt. Bake for 15 minutes until slices become dry. Serve alongside well-chilled avocado dip.

NUTRITIONAL INFO PER SERVING: Calories 269; Fat: 26.7g, Net Carbs: 9.4g, Protein: 2.3g

Vegan Mushroom Pizza

Ready in about: 35 minutes | Serves: 4

INGREDIENTS

2 tsp ghee
1 cup chopped button mushrooms
½ cup sliced mixed colored bell peppers
Pink salt and black pepper to taste

1 almond flour pizza bread
1 cup tomato sauce
1 tsp vegan Parmesan cheese
Vegan Parmesan cheese for garnish

DIRECTIONS

Melt ghee in a skillet over medium heat, sauté the mushrooms and bell peppers for 10 minutes to soften. Season with salt and black pepper. Turn the heat off.

Put the pizza bread on a pizza pan, spread the tomato sauce all over the top and scatter vegetables evenly on top. Season with a little more salt and sprinkle with parmesan cheese.

Bake for 20 minutes until the vegetables are soft and the cheese has melted and is bubbly. Garnish with extra parmesan cheese. Slice pizza and serve with chilled berry juice.

NUTRITIONAL INFO PER SERVING: Calories 295, Fat 20g, Net Carbs 8g, Protein 15g

Grilled Cheese the Keto Way

Ready in about: 15 minutes | Serves: 1

INGREDIENTS

2 eggs

½ tsp baking powder

2 tbsp butter

2 tbsp almond flour

1 ½ tbsp psyllium husk powder

2 ounces cheddar cheese

DIRECTIONS

Whisk together all ingredients except 1 tbsp. butter and cheddar cheese. Place in a square oven-proof bowl, and microwave for 90 seconds. Flip the bun over and cut in half.

Place the cheddar cheese on one half of the bun and top with the other. Melt the remaining butter in a skillet. Add the sandwich and grill until the cheese is melted and the bun is crispy.

NUTRITIONAL INFO PER SERVING: Calories 623, Fat: 51g, Net Carbs: 6.1g, Protein: 25g

Cremini Mushroom Stroganoff

Ready in about: 15 minutes | Serves: 4

INGREDIENTS

3 tbsp butter

1 white onion, chopped

4 cups cremini mushrooms, cubed

2 cups water

½ cup heavy cream

½ cup grated Parmesan cheese

1 ½ tbsp dried mixed herbs

Salt and black pepper to taste

DIRECTIONS

Melt the butter in a saucepan over medium heat, sauté the onion for 3 minutes until soft.

Stir in the mushrooms and cook until tender, about 3 minutes. Add the water, mix, and bring to boil for 4 minutes until the water reduces slightly.

Pour in the heavy cream and parmesan cheese. Stir to melt the cheese. Also, mix in the dried herbs. Season with salt and pepper, simmer for 40 seconds and turn the heat off.

Ladle stroganoff over a bed of spaghetti squash and serve.

NUTRITIONAL INFO PER SERVING: Calories 284, Fat 28g, Net Carbs 1,5g, Protein 8g

Walnut Tofu Sauté

Ready in about: 15 minutes | Serves: 4

INGREDIENTS

1 tbsp olive oil
1 (8 oz) block firm tofu, cubed
1 tbsp tomato paste with garlic and onion
1 tbsp balsamic vinegar

Pink salt and black pepper to taste
½ tsp mixed dried herbs
1 cup chopped raw walnuts

DIRECTIONS

Heat the oil in a skillet over medium heat and cook the tofu for 3 minutes while stirring to brown.

Mix the tomato paste with the vinegar and add to the tofu. Stir, season with salt and black pepper, and cook for another 4 minutes.

Add the herbs and walnuts. Stir and cook on low heat for 3 minutes to be fragrant. Spoon to a side of squash mash and a sweet berry sauce to serve.

NUTRITIONAL INFO PER SERVING: Calories 320, Fat 24g, Net Carbs 4g, Protein 18g

Pumpkin Bake

Ready in about: 45 minutes | Serves: 6

INGREDIENTS

3 large Pumpkins, peeled and sliced
1 cup almond flour
1 cup grated mozzarella cheese

2 tbsp olive oil
½ cup chopped parsley

DIRECTIONS

Preheat the oven to 350ºF. Arrange the pumpkin slices in a baking dish, drizzle with olive oil, and bake for 35 minutes. Mix the almond flour, cheese, and parsley and when the pumpkin is ready, remove it from the oven, and sprinkle the cheese mixture all over. Place back in the oven and grill the top for 5 minutes.

NUTRITIONAL INFO PER SERVING: Calories 125, Fat 4.8g, Net Carbs 5.7g, Protein 2.7g

Stuffed Portobello Mushrooms

Ready in about: 30 minutes | Serves: 2

INGREDIENTS

4 portobello mushrooms, stems removed
2 tbsp olive oil

2 cups lettuce
1 cup crumbled blue cheese

DIRECTIONS

Preheat the oven to 350ºF. Fill the mushrooms with blue cheese and place on a lined baking sheet; bake for 20 minutes. Serve with lettuce drizzled with olive oil.

NUTRITIONAL INFO PER SERVING: Calories 334, Fat: 29g, Net Carbs: 5.5g, Protein: 14g

Vegan Cheesy Chips with Tomatoes

Ready in about: 15 minutes | Serves: 6

INGREDIENTS

5 tomatoes, sliced
¼ cup olive oil

1 tbsp seasoning mix

For Vegan cheese

½ cup pepitas seeds
1 tbsp nutritional yeast

Salt and black pepper, to taste
1 tsp garlic puree

DIRECTIONS

Over the sliced tomatoes, drizzle olive oil. Set oven to 200ºF.

In a food processor, add all vegan cheese ingredients and pulse until the desired consistency is attained. Combine vegan cheese and seasoning mixture. Toss in seasoned tomato slices to coat.

Set the tomato slices on the prepared baking pan and bake for 10 minutes.

NUTRITIONAL INFO PER SERVING: Calories 161; Fat: 14g, Net Carbs: 7.2g, Protein: 4.6g

Tasty Cauliflower Dip

Ready in about: 10 minutes | Serves: 4

INGREDIENTS

¾ pound cauliflower, cut into florets
¼ cup olive oil
Salt and black pepper, to taste
1 garlic clove, smashed

1 tbsp sesame paste
1 tbsp fresh lime juice
½ tsp garam masala

DIRECTIONS

Steam cauliflower until tender for 7 minutes in. Transfer to a blender and pulse until you attain a rice-like consistency.

Place in Garam Masala, oil, black paper, fresh lime juice, garlic, salt, and sesame paste. Blend the mixture until well combined. Decorate with some additional olive oil and serve. Otherwise, refrigerate until ready to use.

NUTRITIONAL INFO PER SERVING: Calories 100; Fat: 8.2g, Net Carbs: 4.7g, Protein: 3.7g

Morning Coconut Smoothie

Ready in about: 5 minutes | Serves: 4

INGREDIENTS

½ cup water
1 ½ cups coconut milk
1 cup frozen cherries

4 cup fresh blueberries
¼ tsp vanilla extract
1 tbsp vegan protein powder

DIRECTIONS

Using a blender, combine all the ingredients and blend well until you attain a uniform and creamy consistency. Divide in glasses and serve!

NUTRITIONAL INFO PER SERVING: Calories 247; Fat: 21.7g, Net Carbs: 14.9g, Protein: 2.6g

Garlicky Bok Choy

Ready in about: 25 minutes | Serves: 4

INGREDIENTS

2 pounds bok choy, chopped
2 tbsp almond oil
1 tsp garlic, minced

½ tsp thyme
½ tsp red pepper flakes, crushed
Salt and black pepper, to the taste

DIRECTIONS

Add Bok choy in a pot containing salted water and cook for 10 minutes over medium heat. Drain and set aside. Place a sauté pan over medium-high heat and warm the oil.

Add in garlic and cook until soft. Stir in the Bok choy, red pepper, black pepper, salt, and thyme and ensure they are heated through. Add more seasonings if needed and serve warm with cauli rice.

NUTRITIONAL INFO PER SERVING: Calories 118; Fat: 7g, Net Carbs: 13.4g, Protein: 2.9g

Avocado and Tomato Burritos

Ready in about: 5 minutes | Serves: 4

INGREDIENTS

2 cups cauli rice
Water for sprinkling
6 zero carb flatbread

2 cups sour cream sauce
1 ½ cups tomato herb salsa
2 avocados, peeled, pitted, sliced

DIRECTIONS

Pour the cauli rice in a bowl, sprinkle with water, and soften in the microwave for 2 minutes.

On flatbread, spread the sour cream all over and distribute the salsa on top. Top with cauli rice and scatter the avocado evenly on top. Fold and tuck the burritos and cut into two.

NUTRITIONAL INFO PER SERVING: Calories 303, Fat 25g, Net Carbs 6g, Protein 8g

Spiced Cauliflower & Peppers

Ready in about: 35 minutes | Serves: 4

INGREDIENTS

1 pound cauliflower, cut into florets
2 bell peppers, halved
¼ cup olive oil

Sea salt and black pepper, to taste
½ tsp cayenne pepper
1 tsp curry powder

DIRECTIONS

Set oven to 425 ºF. Line a parchment paper to a large baking sheet. Sprinkle olive oil to the peppers and cauliflower alongside curry powder, black pepper, salt, and cayenne pepper.

Set the vegetables on the baking sheet. Roast for 30 minutes as you toss in intervals until they start to brown. Serve alongside mushroom pate or homemade tomato dip!

NUTRITIONAL INFO PER SERVING: Calories 166; Fat: 13.9g, Net Carbs: 7.4g, Protein: 3g

Coconut Cauliflower & Parsnip Soup

Ready in about: 20 minutes | Serves: 4

INGREDIENTS

4 cups vegetable broth
2 heads cauliflower, cut into florets
1 cup parsnip, chopped

1 tbsp coconut oil
1 cup coconut milk
½ tsp red pepper flakes

DIRECTIONS

Add water in a pot set over medium-high heat and bring to a boil. Add in cauliflower florets and parsnip, cook for about 10 minutes. Add in broth and coconut oil. While on low heat, cook for an additional 5 minutes. Transfer the mixture to an immersion blender and puree.

Plate into four separate soup bowls; decorate each with red pepper flakes. Serve while warm.

NUTRITIONAL INFO PER SERVING: Calories 94; Fat: 7.2g, Net Carbs: 7g, Protein: 2.7g

Roasted Brussels Sprouts with Sunflower Seeds

Ready in about: 45 minutes | Serves: 6

INGREDIENTS

Nonstick cooking spray
3 pounds brussels sprouts, halved
¼ cup olive oil

Salt and ground black pepper, to taste
1 tsp sunflower seeds
2 tbsp fresh chives, chopped

DIRECTIONS

Set oven to 390ºF. Apply a nonstick cooking spray to a rimmed baking sheet. Arrange sprout halves on the baking sheet. Shake in black pepper, salt, sunflower seeds, and olive oil.

Roast for 40 minutes, until the cabbage becomes soft. Apply a garnish of fresh chopped chives.

NUTRITIONAL INFO PER SERVING: Calories: 186; Fat 17g, Net Carbs 8g, Protein 2.1g

Cheese Stuffed Avocados

Ready in about: 20 minutes | Serves: 4

INGREDIENTS

3 avocados, halved and pitted, skin on
½ cup feta cheese, crumbled
½ cup cheddar cheese, grated

2 eggs, beaten
Salt and black pepper, to taste
1 tbsp fresh basil, chopped

DIRECTIONS

Set oven to 360ºF. Lay the avocado halves in an ovenproof dish. Using a mixing dish, mix both types of cheeses, pepper, eggs, and salt. Split the mixture equally into the avocado halves. Bake thoroughly for 15 to 17 minutes. Decorate with fresh basil before serving.

NUTRITIONAL INFO PER SERVING: Calories 342; Fat: 30.4g, Net Carbs: 7.5g, Protein: 11.1g

SOUPS, STEW & SALADS

Cobb Egg Salad in Lettuce Cups

Ready in about: 25 minutes | Serves: 4

INGREDIENTS

2 chicken breasts, cut into pieces
1 tbsp olive oil
Salt and black pepper to season
6 large eggs
1 ½ cups water

2 tomatoes, seeded, chopped
6 tbsp Greek yogurt
1 head green lettuce, firm leaves removed
for cups

DIRECTIONS

Preheat oven to 400ºF. Put the chicken pieces in a bowl, drizzle with olive oil, and sprinkle with salt and black pepper. Mix the ingredients until the chicken is well coated with the seasoning.

Put the chicken on a prepared baking sheet and spread out evenly. Slide the baking sheet in the oven and bake the chicken until cooked through and golden brown for 8 minutes, turning once.

Bring the eggs to boil in salted water in a pot over medium heat for 6 minutes. Run the eggs in cold water, peel, and chop into small pieces. Transfer to a salad bowl.

Remove the chicken from the oven when ready and add to the salad bowl. Include the tomatoes and Greek yogurt; mix evenly with a spoon. Layer two lettuce leaves each as cups and fill with two tablespoons of egg salad each. Serve with chilled blueberry juice.

NUTRITIONAL INFO PER SERVING: Calories 325, Fat 24.5g, Net Carbs 4g, Protein 21g

Cream of Thyme Tomato Soup

Ready in about: 20 minutes | Serves: 6

INGREDIENTS

2 tbsp ghee
2 large red onions, diced
½ cup raw cashew nuts, diced
2 (28 oz) cans tomatoes

1 tsp fresh thyme leaves + extra to garnish
1 ½ cups water
Salt and black pepper to taste
1 cup heavy cream

DIRECTIONS

Melt ghee in a pot over medium heat and sauté the onion for 4 minutes until softened. Stir in the tomatoes, thyme, water, cashews, and season with salt and black pepper.

Cover and bring to simmer for 10 minutes until thoroughly cooked.

Open, turn the heat off, and puree the ingredients with an immersion blender. Adjust to taste and stir in the heavy cream. Spoon into soup bowls and serve with low carb parmesan cheese toasts.

NUTRITIONAL INFO PER SERVING: Calories 310, Fat 27g, Net Carbs 3g, Protein 11g

Creamy Cauliflower Soup with Bacon Chips

Ready in about: 25 minutes | Serves: 4

INGREDIENTS

2 tbsp ghee
1 onion, chopped
2 head cauliflower, cut into florets
2 cups water

Salt and black pepper to taste
3 cups almond milk
1 cup shredded white cheddar cheese
3 bacon strips

DIRECTIONS

Melt the ghee in a saucepan over medium heat and sauté the onion for 3 minutes until fragrant.

Include the cauli florets, sauté for 3 minutes to slightly soften, add the water, and season with salt and black pepper. Bring to a boil, and then reduce the heat to low. Cover and cook for 10 minutes.

Puree cauliflower with an immersion blender until the ingredients are evenly combined and stir in the almond milk and cheese until the cheese melts. Adjust taste with salt and black pepper.

In a non-stick skillet over high heat, fry the bacon, until crispy. Divide soup between serving bowls, top with crispy bacon, and serve hot.

NUTRITIONAL INFO PER SERVING: Calories 402, Fat 37g, Net Carbs 6g, Protein 8g

Coconut, Green Beans, and Shrimp Curry Soup

Ready in about: 20 minutes | Serves: 4

INGREDIENTS

2 tbsp ghee
1 lb jumbo shrimp, peeled and deveined
2 tsp ginger-garlic puree
2 tbsp red curry paste

6 oz coconut milk
Salt and chili pepper to taste
1 bunch green beans, halved

DIRECTIONS

Melt ghee in a medium saucepan over medium heat. Add the shrimp, season with salt and pepper, and cook until they are opaque, 2 to 3 minutes. Remove shrimp to a plate. Add the ginger-garlic puree and red curry paste to the ghee and sauté for 2 minutes until fragrant.

Stir in the coconut milk; add the shrimp, salt, chili pepper, and green beans. Cook for 4 minutes. Reduce the heat to a simmer and cook an additional 3 minutes, occasionally stirring. Adjust taste with salt, fetch soup into serving bowls, and serve with cauli rice.

NUTRITIONAL INFO PER SERVING: Calories 375, Fat 35.4g, Net Carbs 2g, Protein 9g

Creamy Cauliflower Soup with Chorizo Sausage

Ready in about: 40 minutes | Serves: 4

INGREDIENTS

1 cauliflower head, chopped
1 turnip, chopped
3 tbsp butter
1 chorizo sausage, sliced

2 cups chicken broth
1 small onion, chopped
2 cups water
Salt and black pepper, to taste

DIRECTIONS

Melt 2 tbsp. of the butter in a large pot over medium heat. Stir in onion and cook until soft and golden, about 3-4 minutes. Add cauliflower and turnip, and cook for another 5 minutes.

Pour the broth and water over. Bring to a boil, simmer covered, and cook for about 20 minutes until the vegetables are tender. Remove from heat. Melt the remaining butter in a skillet. Add the chorizo sausage and cook for 5 minutes until crispy. Puree the soup with a hand blender until smooth. Taste and adjust the seasonings. Serve the soup in deep bowls topped with the chorizo sausage.

NUTRITIONAL INFO PER SERVING: Calories 251, Fat: 19.1g, Net Carbs: 5.7g, Protein: 10g

Shrimp with Avocado & Cauliflower Salad

Ready in about: 30 minutes | Serves: 6

INGREDIENTS

1 cauliflower head, florets only
1 pound medium shrimp
¼ cup + 1 tbsp olive oil
1 avocado, chopped

3 tbsp chopped dill
¼ cup lemon juice
2 tbsp lemon zest

DIRECTIONS

Heat 1 tbsp olive oil in a skillet and cook the shrimp until opaque, about 8-10 minutes. Place the cauliflower florets in a microwave-safe bowl, and microwave for 5 minutes. Place the shrimp, cauliflower, and avocado in a large bowl.

Whisk together the remaining olive oil, lemon zest, juice, dill, and some salt and pepper, in another bowl. Pour the dressing over, toss to combine and serve immediately.

NUTRITIONAL INFO PER SERVING: Calories 214, Fat: 17g, Net Carbs: 5g, Protein: 15g

Crispy Bacon Salad with Mozzarella & Tomato

Ready in about: 10 minutes | Serves: 2

INGREDIENTS

1 large tomato, sliced
4 basil leaves
8 mozzarella cheese slices
2 tsp olive oil

6 bacon slices, chopped
1 tsp balsamic vinegar
Sea salt, to taste

DIRECTIONS

Place the bacon in a skillet over medium heat and cook until crispy. Divide the tomato slices between two serving plates. Arrange the mozzarella slices over and top with the basil leaves. Add the crispy bacon on top, drizzle with olive oil and vinegar. Sprinkle with sea salt and serve.

NUTRITIONAL INFO PER SERVING: Calories 279, Fat: 26g, Net Carbs: 1.5g, Protein: 21g

Thyme & Wild Mushroom Soup

Ready in about: 25 minutes | Serves: 4

INGREDIENTS

¼ cup butter
½ cup crème fraiche
12 oz wild mushrooms, chopped
2 tsp thyme leaves

2 garlic cloves, minced
4 cups chicken broth
Salt and black pepper, to taste

DIRECTIONS

Melt the butter in a large pot over medium heat. Add garlic and cook for one minute until tender. Add mushrooms, salt and pepper, and cook for 10 minutes. Pour the broth over and bring to a boil.

Reduce the heat and simmer for 10 minutes. Puree the soup with a hand blender until smooth. Stir in crème Fraiche. Garnish with thyme leaves before serving.

NUTRITIONAL INFO PER SERVING: Calories 281, Fat: 25g, Net Carbs: 5.8g, Protein: 6.1g

Green Minestrone Soup

Ready in about: 25 minutes | Serves: 4

INGREDIENTS

2 tbsp ghee
2 tbsp onion garlic puree
2 heads broccoli, cut in florets
2 stalks celery, chopped

5 cups vegetable broth
1 cup baby spinach
Salt and black pepper to taste

DIRECTIONS

Melt the ghee in a saucepan over medium heat and sauté the garlic for 3 minutes until softened. Mix in the broccoli and celery, and cook for 4 minutes until slightly tender. Pour in the broth, bring to a boil, then reduce the heat to medium-low and simmer covered for about 5 minutes.

Drop in the spinach to wilt, adjust the seasonings, and cook for 4 minutes. Ladle soup into serving bowls and serve with a sprinkle of grated Gruyere cheese and freshly baked low carb carrot bread.

NUTRITIONAL INFO PER SERVING: Calories 227, Fat 20.3g, Net Carbs 2g, Protein 8g

Mediterranean Salad

Ready in about: 10 minutes | Serves: 4

INGREDIENTS

3 tomatoes, sliced
1 large avocado, sliced
8 kalamata olives

¼ lb buffalo mozzarella cheese, sliced
2 tbsp pesto sauce
2 tbsp olive oil

DIRECTIONS

Arrange the tomato slices on a serving platter and place the avocado slices in the middle.
Arrange the olives around the avocado slices and drop pieces of mozzarella on the platter.
Drizzle the pesto sauce all over, and drizzle olive oil as well.

NUTRITIONAL INFO PER SERVING: Calories 290, Fat: 25g, Net Carbs: 4.3g, Protein: 9g

Green Salad with Bacon and Blue Cheese

Ready in about: 15 minutes | Serves: 4

INGREDIENTS

2 (8 oz) pack mixed salad greens
8 strips bacon
1 ½ cups crumbled blue cheese

1 tbsp white wine vinegar
3 tbsp extra virgin olive oil
Salt and black pepper to taste

DIRECTIONS

Pour the salad greens in a salad bowl; set aside. Fry bacon strips in a skillet over medium
heat for 6 minutes, until browned and crispy. Chop the bacon and scatter over the salad.
Add in half of the cheese, toss and set aside.

In a small bowl, whisk the white wine vinegar, olive oil, salt, and black pepper until
dressing is well combined. Drizzle half of the dressing over the salad, toss, and top with
remaining cheese. Divide salad into four plates and serve with crusted chicken fries along
with remaining dressing.

NUTRITIONAL INFO PER SERVING: Calories 205, Fat 20g, Net Carbs 2g, Protein 4g

Caesar Salad with Smoked Salmon and Poached Eggs

Ready in about: 15 minutes | Serves: 4

INGREDIENTS

3 cups water
8 eggs
2 cups torn romaine lettuce

½ cup chopped smoked salmon
6 slices bacon
2 tbsp heinz low carb caesar dressing

DIRECTIONS

Boil the water in a pot over medium heat for 5 minutes and bring to simmer. Crack each egg into a small bowl and gently slide into the water. Poach for 2 to 3 minutes, remove with a perforated spoon, transfer to a paper towel to dry, and plate. Poach the remaining 7 eggs.

Put the bacon in a skillet and fry over medium heat until browned and crispy, about 6 minutes, turning once. Remove, allow cooling, and chop in small pieces.

Toss the lettuce, smoked salmon, bacon, and caesar dressing in a salad bowl. Divide the salad into 4 plates, top with two eggs each, and serve immediately or chilled.

NUTRITIONAL INFO PER SERVING: Calories 260, Fat 21g, Net Carbs 5g, Protein 8g

Brussels Sprouts Salad with Pecorino Romano

Ready in about: 35 minutes | Serves: 6

INGREDIENTS

2 lb Brussels sprouts, halved
3 tbsp olive oil
Salt and black pepper to taste
2 ½ tbsp balsamic vinegar

¼ red cabbage, shredded
1 tbsp Dijon mustard
1 cup grated pecorino romano

DIRECTIONS

Preheat oven to 400ºF and line a baking sheet with foil. Toss the brussels sprouts with olive oil, a little salt, black pepper, and balsamic vinegar, in a bowl, and spread on the baking sheet in an even layer. Bake until tender on the inside and crispy on the outside, about 20 to 25 minutes.

Transfer to a salad bowl and add the red cabbage, Dijon mustard and half of the cheese. Mix until well combined. Sprinkle with the remaining cheese, share the salad onto serving plates, and serve with syrup-grilled salmon.

NUTRITIONAL INFO PER SERVING: Calories 210, Fat 18g, Net Carbs 6g, Protein 4g

Pork Burger Salad with Yellow Cheddar

Ready in about: 25 minutes | Serves: 4

INGREDIENTS

1 lb ground pork
Salt and black pepper to season
1 tbsp olive oil
2 hearts romaine lettuce, torn into pieces

2 firm tomatoes, sliced
¼ red onion, sliced
3 oz yellow cheddar cheese, shredded

DIRECTIONS

Season the pork with salt and black pepper, mix and make medium-sized patties out of them.

Heat the oil in a skillet over medium heat and fry the patties on both sides for 10 minutes until browned and cook within. Transfer to a wire rack to drain oil. When cooled, cut into quarters.

Mix the lettuce, tomatoes, and onion in a salad bowl, season with a little oil, salt, and pepper. Toss and add the pork on top.

Melt the cheese in the microwave for about 90 seconds. Drizzle the cheese over the salad and serve.

NUTRITIONAL INFO PER SERVING: Calories 310, Fat 23g, Net Carbs 2g, Protein 22g

Strawberry Salad with Spinach, Cheese & Almonds

Ready in about: 20 minutes | Serves: 2

INGREDIENTS

4 cups spinach
4 strawberries, sliced
½ cup flaked almonds

1 ½ cup grated hard goat cheese
4 tbsp raspberry vinaigrette
Salt and black pepper, to taste

DIRECTIONS

Preheat your oven to 400ºF. Arrange the grated goat cheese in two circles on two pieces of parchment paper. Place in the oven and bake for 10 minutes.

Find two same bowls, place them upside down, and carefully put the parchment paper on top to give the cheese a bowl-like shape. Let cool that way for 15 minutes. Divide spinach among the bowls and drizzle with vinaigrette. Top with almonds and strawberries.

NUTRITIONAL INFO PER SERVING: Calories 445, Fat: 34.2g, Net Carbs: 5.3g, Protein: 33g

Chicken Creamy Soup

Ready in about: 15 minutes | Serves: 4

INGREDIENTS

2 cups cooked and shredded chicken
3 tbsp butter, melted
4 cups chicken broth
4 tbsp chopped cilantro

¼ cup buffalo sauce
½ cup cream cheese
Salt and black pepper, to taste

DIRECTIONS

Blend the butter, buffalo sauce, and cream cheese, in a food processor, until smooth. Transfer to a pot, add the chicken broth and heat until hot but do not bring to a boil. Stir in chicken and cook until heated through. When ready, remove to soup bowls and serve garnished with cilantro.

NUTRITIONAL INFO PER SERVING: Calories 406, Fat: 29.5g, Net Carbs: 5g, Protein: 26.5g

Grilled Steak Salad with Pickled Peppers

Ready in about: 15 minutes | Serves: 4

INGREDIENTS

1 lb skirt steak, sliced
Salt and black pepper to season
1 tsp olive oil
1 ½ cups mixed salad greens

3 chopped pickled peppers
2 tbsp red wine vinaigrette
½ cup crumbled queso fresco

DIRECTIONS

Brush the steaks with olive oil and season with salt and pepper on both sides.

Heat frying pan over high heat and cook the steaks on each side to the desired doneness, for about 5-6 minutes. Remove to a bowl, cover and leave to rest while you make the salad.

Mix the salad greens, pickled peppers, and vinaigrette in a salad bowl. Add the beef and sprinkle with cheese. Serve the salad with roasted parsnips.

NUTRITIONAL INFO PER SERVING: Calories 315, Fat 26g, Net Carbs 2g, Protein 18g

SIDE DISHES & SNACKS

Parmesan Crackers with Guacamole

Ready in about: 10 minutes | Serves: 4

INGREDIENTS

1 cup finely grated Parmesan cheese
¼ tsp sweet paprika
¼ tsp garlic powder

2 soft avocados, pitted and scooped
1 tomato, chopped
Salt to taste

DIRECTIONS

To make the chips, preheat oven to 350ºF and line a baking sheet with parchment paper.

Mix parmesan cheese, paprika, and garlic powder evenly. Spoon 6 to 8 teaspoons on the baking sheet creating spaces between each mound. Flatten mounds with your hands. Bake for 5 minutes, cool, and remove with a spatula onto a plate.

To make the guacamole, mash avocado, with a fork in a bowl, add in tomato and continue to mash until mostly smooth. Season with salt. Serve crackers with guacamole.

NUTRITIONAL INFO PER SERVING: Calories 229, Fat 20g, Net Carbs 2g, Protein 10g

Cheesy Green Bean Crisps

Ready in about: 30 minutes | Serves: 6

INGREDIENTS

Cooking spray
¼ cup shredded pecorino romano cheese
¼ cup pork rind crumbs
1 tsp garlic powder

Salt and black pepper to taste
2 eggs
1 lb green beans, thread removed

DIRECTIONS

Preheat oven to 425ºF and line two baking sheets with foil. Grease with cooking spray and set aside.

Mix the pecorino, pork rinds, garlic powder, salt, and black pepper in a bowl. Beat the eggs in another bowl. Coat green beans in eggs, then cheese mixture and arrange evenly on the baking sheets.

Grease lightly with cooking spray and bake for 15 minutes to be crispy. Transfer to a wire rack to cool before serving. Serve with sugar-free tomato dip.

NUTRITIONAL INFO PER SERVING: Calories 210, Fat 19g, Net Carbs 3g, Protein 5g

Crunchy Pork Rind and Zucchini Sticks

Ready in about: 20 minutes | Serves: 4

INGREDIENTS

Cooking spray
¼ cup pork rind crumbs
1 tsp sweet paprika
¼ cup shredded Parmesan cheese

Salt and chili pepper to taste
3 fresh eggs
2 zucchinis, cut into strips

DIRECTIONS

Preheat oven to 425ºF and line a baking sheet with foil. Grease with cooking spray and set aside. Mix the pork rinds, paprika, parmesan cheese, salt, and chili pepper in a bowl.

Beat the eggs in another bowl. Coat zucchini strips in egg, then in parmesan mixture, and arrange on the baking sheet. Grease lightly with cooking spray and bake for 15 minutes to be crispy.

To make the aioli, combine in a bowl mayonnaise, lemon juice, and garlic, and gently stir until everything is well incorporated. Add the lemon zest, adjust the seasoning and stir again. Cover and place in the refrigerator until ready to serve.

Arrange the zucchini strips on a serving plate and serve with garlic aioli for dipping.

NUTRITIONAL INFO PER SERVING: Calories 180, Fat 14g, Net Carbs 2g, Protein 6g

Devilled Eggs with Sriracha Mayo

Ready in about: 15 minutes | Serves: 4

INGREDIENTS

8 large eggs
3 cups water
Ice water bath
3 tbsp sriracha sauce

4 tbsp mayonnaise
Salt to taste
¼ tsp smoked paprika

DIRECTIONS

Bring eggs to boil in salted water in a pot over high heat, and then reduce the heat to simmer for 10 minutes. Transfer eggs to an ice water bath, let cool completely and peel the shells.

Slice the eggs in half height wise and empty the yolks into a bowl. Smash with a fork and mix in sriracha sauce, mayonnaise, and half of the paprika until smooth.

Spoon filling into a piping bag with a round nozzle and fill the egg whites to be slightly above the brim. Garnish with remaining paprika and serve immediately.

NUTRITIONAL INFO PER SERVING: Calories 195, Fat 19g, Net Carbs 1g, Protein 4g

Bacon Mashed Cauliflower

Ready in about: 40 minutes | Serves: 6

INGREDIENTS

6 slices bacon
3 heads cauliflower, leaves removed
2 cups water
2 tbsp melted butter

½ cup buttermilk
Salt and black pepper to taste
¼ cup grated yellow cheddar cheese
2 tbsp chopped chives

DIRECTIONS

Preheat oven to 350ºF. Fry bacon in a heated skillet over medium heat for 5 minutes until crispy. Remove to a paper towel-lined plate, allow to cool, and crumble. Set aside and keep bacon fat.

Boil cauli heads in water in a pot over high heat for 7 minutes, until tender. Drain and put in a bowl.

Include butter, buttermilk, salt, black pepper, and puree using a hand blender until smooth and creamy. Lightly grease a casserole dish with the bacon fat and spread the mash in it.

Sprinkle with cheddar cheese and place under the broiler for 4 minutes on high until the cheese melts. Remove and top with bacon and chopped chives. Serve with pan-seared scallops.

NUTRITIONAL INFO PER SERVING: Calories 312, Fat 25g, Net Carbs 6g, Protein 14g

Duo-Cheese Chicken Bake

Ready in about: 30 minutes | Serves: 6

INGREDIENTS

2 tbsp olive oil
8 oz cream cheese
1 lb ground chicken

1 cup buffalo sauce
1 cup ranch dressing
3 cups grated yellow cheddar cheese

DIRECTIONS

Preheat oven to 350ºF. Lightly grease a baking sheet with a cooking spray. Warm the oil in a skillet over medium heat and brown the chicken for a couple of minutes, take off the heat, and set aside.

Spread cream cheese at the bottom of the baking sheet, top with chicken, pour buffalo sauce over, add ranch dressing, and sprinkle with cheddar cheese. Bake for 23 minutes until cheese has melted and golden brown on top. Remove and serve with veggie sticks or low carb crackers.

NUTRITIONAL INFO PER SERVING: Calories 216, Fat 16g, Net Carbs 3g, Protein 14g

Balsamic Brussels Sprouts with Prosciutto

Ready in about: 45 minutes | Serves: 4

INGREDIENTS

3 tbsp balsamic vinegar
1 tbsp erythritol
½ tbsp olive oil

Salt and black pepper to taste
1 lb Brussels sprouts, halved
5 slices prosciutto, chopped

DIRECTIONS

Preheat oven to 400ºF and line a baking sheet with parchment paper. Mix balsamic vinegar, erythritol, olive oil, salt, and black pepper and combine with the brussels sprouts in a bowl.

Spread the mixture on the baking sheet and roast for 30 minutes until tender on the inside and crispy on the outside. Toss with prosciutto, share among 4 plates, and serve with chicken breasts.

NUTRITIONAL INFO PER SERVING: Calories 166, Fat 14g, Net Carbs 0g, Protein 8g

Buttery Herb Roasted Radishes

Ready in about: 25 minutes | Serves: 6

INGREDIENTS

2 lb small radishes, greens removed
3 tbsp olive oil
Salt and black pepper to season

3 tbsp unsalted butter
1 tbsp chopped parsley
1 tbsp chopped tarragon

DIRECTIONS

Preheat oven to 400ºF and line a baking sheet with parchment paper. Toss radishes with oil, salt, and black pepper. Spread on baking sheet and roast for 20 minutes until browned.

Heat butter in a large skillet over medium heat to brown and attain a nutty aroma, 2 to 3 minutes.

Take out the parsnips from the oven and transfer to a serving plate. Pour over the browned butter atop and sprinkle with parsley and tarragon. Serve with roasted rosemary chicken.

NUTRITIONAL INFO PER SERVING: Calories 160, Fat 14g, Net Carbs 2g, Protein 5g

Bacon-Wrapped Jalapeño Peppers

Ready in about: 30 minutes | Serves: 6

INGREDIENTS

12 jalapeños
¼ cup shredded colby cheese

6 oz cream cheese, softened
6 slices bacon, halved

DIRECTIONS

Cut the jalapeno peppers in half, and then remove the membrane and seeds. Combine cheeses and stuff into the pepper halves. Wrap each pepper with a bacon strip and secure with toothpicks.

Place the filled peppers on a baking sheet lined with a piece of foil. Bake at 350ºF for 25 minutes until bacon has browned, and crispy and cheese is golden brown on the top. Remove to a paper towel lined plate to absorb grease, arrange on a serving plate, and serve warm.

NUTRITIONAL INFO PER SERVING: Calories 206, Fat 17g, Net Carbs 0g, Protein 14g

Parmesan Crackers

Ready in about: 25 minutes | Serves: 6

INGREDIENTS

1 ¼ cups coconut flour
1 ¼ cup grated Parmesan cheese
Salt and black pepper to taste
1 tsp garlic powder

¼ cup butter, softened
¼ tsp sweet paprika
½ cup heavy cream
Water as needed

DIRECTIONS

Preheat the oven to 350ºF.

Mix the coconut flour, parmesan cheese, salt, pepper, garlic powder, and paprika in a bowl. Add in the butter and mix well. Top with the heavy cream and mix again until a smooth, thick mixture has formed. Add 1 to 2 tablespoon of water at this point, if it is too thick.

Place the dough on a cutting board and cover with plastic wrap. Use a rolling pin to spread out the dough into a light rectangle. Cut cracker squares out of the dough and arrange them on a baking sheet without overlapping. Bake for 20 minutes and transfer to a serving bowl after.

NUTRITIONAL INFO PER SERVING: Calories 115, Fat 3g, Net Carbs 0.7g, Protein 5g

Spicy Chicken Cucumber Bites

Ready in about: 5 minutes | Serves: 6

INGREDIENTS

2 cucumbers, sliced with a 3-inch thickness
2 cups small dices leftover chicken
¼ jalapeño, seeded and minced

1 tbsp Dijon mustard
¼ cup mayonnaise
Salt and black pepper to taste

DIRECTIONS

Cut mid-level holes in cucumber slices with a knife and set aside. Combine chicken, jalapeno, mustard, mayonnaise, salt, and black pepper to be evenly mixed. Fill cucumber holes with chicken mixture and serve.

NUTRITIONAL INFO PER SERVING: Calories 170, Fat 14g, Net Carbs 0g, Protein 10g

Turkey Pastrami & Mascarpone Cheese Pinwheels

Ready in about: 40 minutes | Serves: 4

INGREDIENTS

Cooking spray
8 oz mascarpone cheese
10 oz turkey pastrami, sliced

10 canned pepperoncini peppers, sliced and drained

DIRECTIONS

Lay a 12 x 12 plastic wrap on a flat surface and arrange the pastrami all over slightly overlapping each other. Spread the cheese on top of the salami layers and arrange the pepperoncini on top.

Hold two opposite ends of the plastic wrap and roll the pastrami. Twist both ends to tighten and refrigerate for 2 hours. Unwrap the salami roll and slice into 2-inch pinwheels. Serve.

NUTRITIONAL INFO PER SERVING: Calories 266, Fat 24g, Net Carbs 0g, Protein 13g

Spinach and Ricotta Gnocchi

Ready in about: 13 minutes | Serves: 4

INGREDIENTS

3 cups chopped spinach
1 cup ricotta cheese
¼ tsp nutmeg powder
1 egg, cracked into a bowl

Salt and black pepper
Almond flour, on standby
2 ½ cups water
2 tbsp butter

DIRECTIONS

To a bowl, add the ricotta cheese, half of the parmesan cheese, egg, nutmeg powder, salt, spinach, and pepper. Mix well. Make quenelles of the mixture using two tablespoons and set aside.

Bring the water to boil over high heat on a stovetop, about 5 minutes. Place one gnocchi onto the water, if it breaks apart; add some more flour to the other gnocchi to firm it up.

Put the remaining gnocchi in the water to poach and rise to the top, about 2 minutes. Remove the gnocchi with a perforated spoon to a serving plate. Melt the butter in a microwave and pour over the gnocchi. Sprinkle with the remaining parmesan cheese and serve with a green salad.

NUTRITIONAL INFO PER SERVING: Calories 125, Fat 8.3g, Net Carbs 4.1g, Protein 6.5g

Herb Cheese Sticks

Ready in about: 15 minutes | Serves: 4

INGREDIENTS

1 cup pork rinds, crushed
1 tbsp Italian herb mix
1 egg

1 lb swiss cheese, cut into sticks
Cooking spray

DIRECTIONS

Preheat oven to 350ºF and line a baking sheet with parchment paper. Combine pork rinds and herb mix in a bowl to be evenly mixed and beat the egg in another bowl. Coat the cheese sticks in egg and then dredge in pork rind mixture. Arrange on baking sheet. Bake for 4 minutes, take out after, let cool for 2 minutes, and serve with marinara sauce.

NUTRITIONAL INFO PER SERVING: Calories 188, Fat 17.3g, Net Carbs 0g, Protein 8g

Lemony Fried Artichokes

Ready in about: 20 minutes | Serves: 4

INGREDIENTS

12 fresh baby artichokes
2 tbsp lemon juice

2 tbsp olive oil
Salt to taste

DIRECTIONS

Slice the artichokes vertically into narrow wedges. Drain on paper towels before frying. Heat olive oil in a cast-iron skillet over high heat. Fry the artichokes until browned and crispy. Drain excess oil on paper towels. Sprinkle with salt and lemon juice.

NUTRITIONAL INFO PER SERVING: Calories 35, Fat: 2.4g, Net Carbs: 2.9g, Protein: 2g

Crispy Chorizo with Cheesy Topping

Ready in about: 30 minutes | Serves: 6

INGREDIENTS

7 ounces Spanish chorizo
4 ounces cream cheese

¼ cup chopped parsley

DIRECTIONS

Preheat your oven to 325 ºF. Slice the chorizo into 30 slices

Line a baking dish with waxed paper. Bake the chorizo for 15 minutes until crispy. Remove from the oven and let cool. Arrange on a serving platter. Top each slice with some cream cheese.

Serve sprinkled with chopped parsley.

NUTRITIONAL INFO PER SERVING: Calories 172, Fat: 13g, Net Carbs: 0g, Protein: 5g

Buttered Broccoli

Ready in about: 10 minutes | Serves: 6

INGREDIENTS

1 broccoli head, florets only
Salt to taste

¼ cup butter

DIRECTIONS

Place the broccoli in a pot filled with salted water and bring to a boil. Cook for about 3 minutes.

Melt the butter in a microwave. Drain the broccoli and transfer to a plate. Drizzle the butter over and season with some salt and pepper.

NUTRITIONAL INFO PER SERVING: Calories 114, Fat: 7.8g, Net Carbs: 5.5g, Protein: 3.9g

Boiled Stuffed Eggs

Ready in about: 30 minutes | Serves: 6

INGREDIENTS

6 eggs
1 tbsp green tabasco

¼ cup mayonnaise
Salt to taste

DIRECTIONS

Place the eggs in a saucepan and cover with salted water. Bring to a boil over medium heat. Boil for 10 minutes. Place the eggs in an ice bath and let cool for 10 minutes.

Peel and slice in half lengthwise. Scoop out the yolks to a bowl; mash with a fork. Whisk together the tabasco, mayonnaise, mashed yolks, and salt, in a bowl. Spoon this mixture into egg white.

NUTRITIONAL INFO PER SERVING: Calories 178, Fat: 17g, Net Carbs: 5g, Protein: 6g

Italian-Style Chicken Wraps

Ready in about: 20 minutes | Serves: 8

INGREDIENTS

¼ tsp garlic powder
8 ounces provolone cheese
8 raw chicken tenders

½ tsp black pepper
8 prosciutto slices

DIRECTIONS

Pound the chicken until half an inch thick. Season with salt, pepper, and garlic powder. Cut the provolone cheese into 8 strips. Place a slice of prosciutto on a flat surface. Place one chicken tender on top. Top with a provolone strip.

Roll the chicken and secure with previously soaked skewers. Grill the wraps for 3 minutes per side.

NUTRITIONAL INFO PER SERVING: Calories 174, Fat: 10g, Net Carbs: 0.7g, Protein: 17g

Party Bacon and Pistachio Balls

Ready in about: 45 minutes | Serves: 8

INGREDIENTS

8 bacon slices, cooked and chopped
8 ounces Liverwurst
¼ cup chopped pistachios

1 tsp Dijon mustard
6 ounces cream cheese

DIRECTIONS

Combine the liverwurst and pistachios in the bowl of your food processor. Pulse until smooth. Whisk the cream cheese and mustard in another bowl. Make 12 balls out of the liverwurst mixture.

Make a thin cream cheese layer over. Coat with bacon, arrange on a plate and chill for 30 minutes.

NUTRITIONAL INFO PER SERVING: Calories 145, Fat: 12g, Net Carbs: 1.5g, Protein: 7g

Dill Pickles with Tuna-Mayo Topping

Ready in about: 40 minutes | Serves: 12

INGREDIENTS

18 ounces canned and drained tuna
6 large dill pickles
¼ tsp garlic powder

¼ cup sugar-free mayonnaise
1 tbsp onion flakes

DIRECTIONS

Combine the mayonnaise, tuna, onion flakes, and garlic powder in a bowl. Cut the pickles in half lengthwise. Top each half with tuna mixture. Place in the fridge for 30 minutes before serving.

NUTRITIONAL INFO PER SERVING: Calories 118, Fat: 10g, Net Carbs: 1.5g, Protein: 11g

Mozzarella & Prosciutto Wraps

Ready in about: 15 minutes | Serves: 6

INGREDIENTS

6 thin prosciutto slices
18 basil leaves

18 mozzarella ciliegine

DIRECTIONS

Cut the prosciutto slices into three strips. Place basil leaves at the end of each strip. Top with mozzarella. Wrap the mozzarella in prosciutto. Secure with toothpicks.

NUTRITIONAL INFO PER SERVING: Calories 163, Fat: 12g, Net Carbs: 0.1g, Protein: 13g

Spiced Gruyere Crisps

Ready in about: 10 minutes | Serves: 4

INGREDIENTS

2 cups gruyere cheese, shredded
½ tsp garlic powder
¼ tsp onion powder

1 rosemary sprig, minced
½ tsp chili powder

DIRECTIONS

Set oven to 400ºF. Coat two baking sheets with parchment paper.

Mix Gruyere cheese with the seasonings. Take 1 tablespoon of cheese mixture and form small mounds on the baking sheets. Bake for 6 minutes. Leave to cool. Serve.

NUTRITIONAL INFO PER SERVING: Calories 205; Fat: 15g, Net Carbs: 2.9g, Protein: 14.5g

BRUNCH & DINNER

Homemade Pizza Crust

Ready in about: 8 minutes | Serves: 8

INGREDIENTS

3 cups almond flour
3 tbsp butter, then melted

¼ tsp salt
3 large eggs

DIRECTIONS

Preheat the oven to 350ºF and in a bowl, mix the almond flour, butter, salt, and eggs until a dough forms. Mold the dough into a ball and place in between two wide parchment papers on a flat surface.

Use a rolling pin to roll it out into a circle of a quarter-inch thickness. Slide the pizza dough into the pizza pan and remove the parchment papers. Bake the dough for 20 minutes.

NUTRITIONAL INFO PER SERVING: Calories 151; Fat: 13.1g, Net Carbs: 2.7g, Protein: 7.3g

Goat Cheese Muffins with Ajillo Mushrooms

Ready in about: 45 minutes | Serves: 6

INGREDIENTS

1 ½ cups double cream
5 ounces goat cheese, crumbled
3 eggs, beaten
Salt and black pepper, to taste

1 tbsp butter, softened
2 cups mushrooms, chopped
2 garlic cloves, minced

DIRECTIONS

Preheat the oven to 320ºF. Insert 6 ramekins into a large pan. Add in boiling water up to 1-inch depth.In a pan, over medium heat, warm double cream. Set heat to a simmer; stir in goat cheese and cook until melted.

Set the beaten eggs in a bowl and place in 3 tablespoons of the hot cream mixture; combine well. Place the mixture back to the pan with hot cream/cheese mixture.

Sprinkle with pepper and salt. Ladle the mixture into ramekins. Bake for 40 minutes.

Melt butter in a pan over medium heat. Add garlic and mushrooms, season with salt and pepper and sauté for 5-6 minutes until tender and translucent.

Spread the ajillo mushrooms on top of each cooled muffin to serve.

NUTRITIONAL INFO PER SERVING: Calories 263, Fat: 22.4g, Net Carbs: 6.1g, Protein: 10g

Cheesy Basil Omelet

Ready in about: 10 minutes | Serves: 2

INGREDIENTS

4 slices cooked bacon, crumbled
4 eggs, beaten
1 tsp basil, chopped

1 tsp parsley, chopped
Sea salt and black pepper
½ cup cheddar cheese, grated

DIRECTIONS

In a frying pan, cook the bacon until sizzling. Add in eggs, parsley, black pepper, salt, and rosemary.Scatter the cheese over the half of omelet; using a spatula fold in half over the filling. Cook for 1 extra minute or until cooked through and serve immediately.

NUTRITIONAL INFO PER SERVING: Calories 431; Fat: 33.1g, Net Carbs: 2.7g, Protein: 30.3g

Tuna & Monterey Jack Stuffed Avocado

Ready in about: 20 minutes | Serves: 4

INGREDIENTS

2 avocados, halved and pitted
4 ounces Monterey Jack cheese, grated
2 ounces canned tuna, flaked

2 tbsp chives, chopped
Salt and black pepper, to taste
½ cup curly endive, chopped

DIRECTIONS

Set oven to 360ºF. Set avocado halves in an ovenproof dish. Using a mixing bowl, mix Monterey Jack cheese, chives, pepper, salt, and tuna. Stuff the cheese/tuna mixture in avocado halves.

Bake for 15 minutes or until the top is golden brown. Sprinkle with fresh cilantro and serve with curly endive for garnish.

NUTRITIONAL INFO PER SERVING: Calories: 286; Fat 23.9g, Net Carbs 9g, Protein 11.2g

Spanish Salsa Aioli

Ready in about: 10 minutes | Serves: 8

INGREDIENTS

1 tbsp lemon juice
1 egg yolk, at room temperature
1 clove garlic, crushed
½ tsp salt

½ cup olive oil
¼ tsp black pepper
¼ cup fresh parsley, chopped

DIRECTIONS

Using a blender, place in salt, vinegar, garlic, and egg yolk; pulse well to get a smooth and creamy mixture. Set blender to slow speed.

Slowly sprinkle in olive oil and combine to ensure the oil incorporates well.

Stir in parsley and black pepper. Refrigerate the mixture until ready.

NUTRITIONAL INFO PER SERVING: Calories 116; Fat: 13.2g, Net Carbs: 0.2g, Protein: 0.4g

Bacon & Eggplant Boats

Ready in about: 35 minutes | Serves: 3

INGREDIENTS

3 eggplants, cut into halves
1 tbsp deli mustard
2 bacon, cooked, crumbled

6 eggs
Salt, to taste + ¼ tsp black pepper
¼ tsp dried parsley

DIRECTIONS

Scoop flesh from eggplant halves to make shells; set the eggplant boats on a greased baking pan. Spread mustard on the bottom of every eggplant half. Split the bacon among eggplant boats.

Crack an egg in each half, sprinkle with parsley, pepper, and salt. Set oven at 400ºF and bake for 30 minutes or until boats become tender.

NUTRITIONAL INFO PER SERVING: Calories 506; Fat 41g, Net Carbs 4.5g, Protein 27.5g

Ham & Egg Mug Cups

Ready in about: 5 minutes | Serves: 2

INGREDIENTS

4 eggs
4 tbsp coconut milk
¼ cup ham, cubed

½ tsp chili pepper
Salt and black pepper, to taste
2 tbsp chives, chopped

DIRECTIONS

Mix all ingredients excluding chives. With a cooking spray, grease two microwave-safe cups. Divide the egg mixture into the cups.

Transfer to the microwave and cook for 1 minute. Decorate with fresh chives before serving.

NUTRITIONAL INFO PER SERVING: Calories: 244; Fat 17.5g, Net Carbs 2.9g, Protein 19.2g

Spicy Cheese Chips

Ready in about: 18 minutes | Serves: 2

INGREDIENTS

3 cups cheddar cheese, grated
¼ tsp salt
½ tsp garlic powder

½ tsp cayenne pepper
½ tsp dried rosemary
¼ tsp chili powder

DIRECTIONS

Set oven to 420ºF. Line a parchment paper on a baking sheet.

Mix grated cheese with spices. Create 2 tablespoons of cheese mixture into small mounds on the baking sheet. Bake for about 15 minutes; allow to cool to harden the chips.

NUTRITIONAL INFO PER SERVING: Calories: 100; Fat 8g, Net Carbs 0g, Protein 7g

Smoked Ham & Egg Muffins

Ready in about: 20 minutes | Serves: 6

INGREDIENTS

24 slices smoked ham
6 eggs, beaten
Salt and black pepper, to taste

¼ cup fresh parsley, chopped
¼ cup ricotta cheese
¼ cup Brie, chopped

DIRECTIONS

Set oven to 390ºF. Line 2 slices of smoked ham to each muffin cup to circle each mold.

In a mixing bowl, mix the rest of the ingredients. Fill ¾ of the ham lined muffin cup with the egg/cheese mixture. Bake for 15 minutes. Serve warm!

NUTRITIONAL INFO PER SERVING: Calories: 268; Fat 18.3g, Net Carbs 0.7g, Protein 26.2g

Baked Chicken Legs with Cheesy Spread

Ready in about: 45 minutes | Serves: 4

INGREDIENTS

4 chicken legs
¼ cup goat cheese
2 tbsp sour cream

1 tbsp butter, softened
1 onion, chopped
Sea salt and black pepper, to taste

DIRECTIONS

Set oven to 360ºF. Bake legs for 25-30 minutes until crispy and browned. In a mixing bowl, mix the rest of the ingredients to form the spread. Serve alongside the chicken legs.

NUTRITIONAL INFO PER SERVING: Calories 119; Fat: 10.5g, Net Carbs: 1.1g, Protein: 5.1g

Bacon Balls with Brie Cheese

Ready in about: 15 minutes | Serves: 5

INGREDIENTS

3 ounces bacon
6 ounces goat's cheese
1 chili pepper, seeded and chopped

¼ tsp parsley flakes
½ tsp paprika

DIRECTIONS

Set a frying pan over medium heat and fry the bacon until crispy; then chop it into small pieces. Place the other ingredients in a bowl and mix to combine well. Refrigerate the mixture. Create balls from the mixture. Set the crushed bacon in a plate. Roll the balls around to coat all sides.

NUTRITIONAL INFO PER SERVING: Calories 206; Fat: 16.5g, Net Carbs: 0.6g, Protein: 13.4g

Chorizo Egg Balls

Ready in about: 35 minutes | Serves: 6

INGREDIENTS

2 eggs
½ cup butter, softened
8 black olives, pitted and chopped
3 tbsp mayonnaise

Salt and crushed red pepper flakes, to taste
3 slices cooked chorizo, chopped
2 tbsp chia seeds

DIRECTIONS

In a food processor, place eggs, olives, pepper, mayonnaise, butter, and salt and blitz until everything is incorporated. Stir in the chopped chorizo. Refrigerate for 30 minutes. Form balls from the mixture.

Set the chia seeds on a serving bowl; roll the balls through to coat. Place in an airtight container and place in the refrigerator for 4 days.

NUTRITIONAL INFO PER SERVING: Calories 174, Fat: 15.2g, Net Carbs: 4.3g, Protein: 5.9g

Crabmeat & Cheese Stuffed Avocado

Ready in about: 25 minutes | Serves: 4

INGREDIENTS

1 tsp olive oil
1 cup crabmeat
2 avocados, halved and pitted

3 ounces cream cheese
¼ cup almonds, chopped
1 tsp smoked paprika

DIRECTIONS

Set oven to 425ºF. Grease oil on a baking pan.

In a bowl, mix crabmeat with cream cheese. To the avocado halves, place in almonds and crabmeat/cheese mixture and bake for 18 minutes. Decorate with smoked paprika and serve.

NUTRITIONAL INFO PER SERVING: Calories 264, Fat: 24.4g, Net Carbs: 11g, Protein: 3.7g

Pureed Broccoli with Roquefort Cheese

Ready in about: 15 minutes | Serves: 4

INGREDIENTS

1 ½ pounds broccoli, broken into florets
2 tbsp olive oil, divided
1 tsp crushed garlic
1 rosemary sprig, chopped

1 thyme sprig, chopped
2 cups roquefort cheese, crumbled
Black pepper to taste

DIRECTIONS

Place salted water in a deep pan and set over medium heat. Add in broccoli and boil for 8 minutes. Remove the cooked florets to a casserole dish.

In a food processor, pulse ½ of the broccoli. Place in 1 tablespoon of oil and 1 cup of the cooking liquid. Do the same with the remaining water, broccoli, and 1 tablespoon of olive oil. Stir in the remaining ingredients and serve.

NUTRITIONAL INFO PER SERVING: Calories 230, Fat: 17.7g, Net Carbs: 7.2g, Protein: 11.9g

DESSERTS & DRINKS

Blueberry Ice Pops

Ready in about: 5 minutes + cooling time | Serves: 6

INGREDIENTS

3 cups blueberries
½ tbsp lemon juice

¼ cup swerve
¼ cup water

DIRECTIONS

Pour the blueberries, lemon juice, swerve, and water in a blender, and puree on high speed for 2 minutes until smooth. Strain through a sieve into a bowl, discard the solids.

Mix in more water if too thick. Divide the mixture into ice pop molds, insert stick cover, and freeze for 4 hours to 1 week. When ready to serve, dip in warm water and remove the pops.

NUTRITIONAL INFO PER SERVING: Calories 48, Fat 1.2g, Net Carbs 7.9g, Protein 2.3g

Lemon Cheesecake Mousse

Ready in about: 5 minutes +cooling time | Serves: 4

INGREDIENTS

24 oz cream cheese, softened
2 cups swerve confectioner's sugar
2 lemons, juiced and zested

Pink salt to taste
1 cup whipped cream + extra for garnish

DIRECTIONS

Whip the cream cheese in a bowl with a hand mixer until light and fluffy. Mix in the sugar, lemon juice, and salt. Fold in the whipped cream to evenly combine.

Spoon the mousse into serving cups and refrigerate to thicken for 1 hour. Swirl with extra whipped cream and garnish lightly with lemon zest. Serve immediately.

NUTRITIONAL INFO PER SERVING: Calories 223, Fat 18g, Net Carbs 3g, Protein 12g

Coffee Fat Bombs

Ready in about: 3 minutes + cooling time | Serves: 6

INGREDIENTS

1 ½ cups mascarpone cheese
½ cup melted butter
3 tbsp unsweetened cocoa powder

¼ cup erythritol
6 tbsp brewed coffee, room temperature

DIRECTIONS

Whisk the mascarpone cheese, butter, cocoa powder, erythritol, and coffee with a hand mixer until creamy and fluffy, for 1 minute. Fill into muffin tins and freeze for 3 hours until firm.

NUTRITIONAL INFO PER SERVING: Calories 145, Fat 14g, Net Carbs 2g, Protein 4g

Chocolate Chip Cookies

Ready in about: 20 minutes | Serves: 4

INGREDIENTS

1 cup butter, softened
2 cups swerve brown sugar
3 eggs

2 cups almond flour
2 cups unsweetened chocolate chips

DIRECTIONS

Preheat oven to 350ºF and line a baking sheet with parchment paper.

Whisk the butter and sugar with a hand mixer for 3 minutes or until light and fluffy. Add the eggs one at a time, and scrape the sides as you whisk. Mix in the flour in low speed until well combined.

Fold in the chocolate chips. Scoop 3 tablespoons each on the baking sheet creating spaces between each mound and bake for 15 minutes to swell and harden. Remove, cool and serve.

NUTRITIONAL INFO PER SERVING: Calories 317, Fat 27g, Net Carbs 8.9g, Protein 6.3g

Coconut Bars

Ready in about: 3 hours | Serves: 4

INGREDIENTS

3 ½ ounces ghee
10 saffron threads
1 ¼ cups coconut milk

1 ¾ cups shredded coconut
4 tbsp sweetener
1 tsp cardamom powder

DIRECTIONS

Combine the shredded coconut with 1 cup of the coconut milk. In another bowl, mix together the remaining coconut milk with the sweetener and saffron. Let sit for 30 minutes.

Heat the ghee in a wok. Add the coconut mixture as well as the saffron mixture, and cook for 5 minutes on low heat, mixing continuously. Stir in the cardamom and cook for another 5 minutes.

Spread the mixture onto a small container and freeze for 2 hours. Cut into bars and enjoy!

NUTRITIONAL INFO PER SERVING: Calories 215, Fat: 22g, Net Carbs: 1.4g, Protein: 2g

White Chocolate Cheesecake Bites

Ready in about: 4 minutes + cooling time | Serves: 6

INGREDIENTS

10 oz unsweetened white chocolate chips
½ half and half
20 oz cream cheese, softened

½ cup swerve
1 tsp vanilla extract

DIRECTIONS

In a saucepan, melt the chocolate with half and a half on low heat for 1 minute. Turn the heat off. In a bowl, whisk the cream cheese, swerve, and vanilla extract with a hand mixer until smooth. Stir into the chocolate mixture. Spoon into silicone muffin tins and freeze for 4 hours until firm.

NUTRITIONAL INFO PER SERVING: Calories 241, Fat 22g, Net Carbs 3.1g, Protein 5g

Strawberry Vanilla Shake

Ready in about: 2 minutes | Serves: 4

INGREDIENTS

2 cups strawberries, stemmed and halved
12 strawberries to garnish
½ cup cold unsweetened almond milk

2/3 tsp vanilla extract
½ cup heavy whipping cream
2 tbsp swerve

DIRECTIONS

Process the strawberries, milk, vanilla extract, whipping cream, and swerve in a large blender for 2 minutes; work in two batches if needed . The shake should be frosty.

Pour into glasses, stick in straws, garnish with strawberry halves, and serve.

NUTRITIONAL INFO PER SERVING: Calories 285, Fat 22.6g, Net Carbs 3.1g, Protein 16g

Chia and Blackberry Pudding

Ready in about: 10 minutes | Serves: 2

INGREDIENTS

1 cup full-fat natural yogurt
2 tsp swerve
2 tbsp chia seeds

1 cup fresh blackberries
1 tbsp lemon zest
Mint leaves, to serve

DIRECTIONS

Mix together the yogurt and the swerve. Stir in the chia seeds. Reserve 4 blackberries for garnish and mash the remaining ones with a fork until pureed. Stir in the yogurt mixture

Chill in the fridge for 30 minutes. When cooled, divide the mixture between 2 glasses. Top each with a couple of raspberries, mint leaves and serve.

NUTRITIONAL INFO PER SERVING: Calories 169, Fat: 10g, Net Carbs: 4.7g, Protein: 7.5g

Cranberry White Chocolate Barks

Ready in about: 5 minutes | Serves: 6

INGREDIENTS

10 oz unsweetened white chocolate, chopped
½ cup erythritol

¼ cup dried cranberries, chopped
¼ cup toasted walnuts, chopped
¼ tsp pink salt

DIRECTIONS

Line a baking sheet with parchment paper. Pour chocolate and erythritol in a bowl, and melt in the microwave for 25 seconds, stirring three times until fully melted. Stir in the cranberries, walnuts, and salt, reserving a few cranberries and walnuts for garnishing.

Pour the mixture on the baking sheet and spread out. Sprinkle with remaining cranberries and walnuts. Refrigerate for 2 hours to set. Break into bite-size pieces to serve.

NUTRITIONAL INFO PER SERVING: Calories 225, Fat 21g, Net Carbs 3g, Protein 6g

Peanut Butter Ice Cream

Ready in about: 50 minutes + cooling time | Serves: 4

INGREDIENTS

½ cup smooth peanut butter
½ cup swerve
3 cups half and half

1 tsp vanilla extract
2 pinches salt

DIRECTIONS

Beat peanut butter and swerve in a bowl with a hand mixer until smooth. Gradually whisk in half and half until thoroughly combined. Mix in vanilla and salt. Pour mixture into a loaf pan and freeze for 45 minutes until firmed up. Scoop into glasses when ready to eat and serve.

NUTRITIONAL INFO PER SERVING: Calories 290, Fat 23g, Net Carbs 6g, Protein 13g

Blackcurrant Iced Tea

Ready in about: 8 minutes | Serves: 4

INGREDIENTS

6 unflavored tea bags
2 cups water
½ cup sugar-free blackcurrant extract

Swerve to taste
Ice cubes for serving
Lemon slices to garnish, cut on the side

DIRECTIONS

Pour the ice cubes in a pitcher and place it in the fridge.

Bring the water to boil in a saucepan over medium heat for 3 minutes and turn the heat off. Stir in the sugar to dissolve and steep the tea bags in the water for 2 minutes.

Remove the bags after and let the tea cool down. Stir in the blackcurrant extract until well incorporated, remove the pitcher from the fridge, and pour the mixture over the ice cubes.

Let sit for 3 minutes to cool and after, pour the mixture into tall glasses. Add some more ice cubes, place the lemon slices on the rim of the glasses, and serve the tea cold.

NUTRITIONAL INFO PER SERVING: Calories 22, Fat 0g, Net Carbs 5g, Protein 0g

Almond Butter Fat Bombs

Ready in about: 3 minutes + cooling time | Serves: 4

INGREDIENTS

½ cup almond butter
½ cup coconut oil

4 tbsp unsweetened cocoa powder
½ cup erythritol

DIRECTIONS

Melt butter and coconut oil in the microwave for 45 seconds, stirring twice until properly melted and mixed. Mix in cocoa powder and erythritol until completely combined.

Pour into muffin moulds and refrigerate for 3 hours to harden.

NUTRITIONAL INFO PER SERVING: Calories 193, Fat 18.3g, Net Carbs 2g, Protein 4g

Almond Milk Hot Chocolate

Ready in about: 7 minutes | Serves: 4

INGREDIENTS

3 cups almond milk
4 tbsp unsweetened cocoa powder
2 tbsp swerve

3 tbsp almond butter
Finely chopped almonds to garnish

DIRECTIONS

In a saucepan, add the almond milk, cocoa powder, and swerve. Stir the mixture until the sugar dissolves. Set the pan over low to heat through for 5 minutes, without boiling.

Swirl the mix occasionally. Turn the heat off and stir in the almond butter to be incorporated. Pour the hot chocolate into mugs and sprinkle with chopped almonds. Serve warm.

NUTRITIONAL INFO PER SERVING: Calories 225, Fat 21.5g, Net Carbs 0.6g, Protein 4.5g

Strawberry and Basil Lemonade

Ready in about: 3 minutes | Serves: 4

INGREDIENTS

4 cups water
12 strawberries, leaves removed
1 cup fresh lemon juice
¼ cup fresh basil

¾ cup swerve
Crushed Ice
Halved strawberries to garnish
Basil leaves to garnish

DIRECTIONS

Spoon some ice into 4 serving glasses and set aside. In a pitcher, add the water, strawberries, lemon juice, basil, and swerve. Insert the blender and process the ingredients for 30 seconds.

The mixture should be pink and the basil finely chopped. Adjust the taste and add the ice in the glasses. Drop 2 strawberry halves and some basil in each glass and serve immediately.

NUTRITIONAL INFO PER SERVING: Calories 66, Fat 0.1g, Net Carbs 5.8g, Protein 0.7g

Coconut Fat Bombs

Ready in about: 22 minutes +cooling time | Serves: 4

INGREDIENTS

2/3 cup coconut oil, melted
1 (14 oz) can coconut milk

18 drops stevia liquid
1 cup unsweetened coconut flakes

DIRECTIONS

Mix the coconut oil with the milk and stevia to combine. Stir in the coconut flakes until well distributed. Pour into silicone muffin molds and freeze for 1 hour to harden.

NUTRITIONAL INFO PER SERVING: Calories 214, Fat 19g, Net Carbs 2g, Protein 4g

Mixed Berry Nuts Mascarpone Bowl

Ready in about: 8 minutes | Serves: 4

INGREDIENTS

4 cups Greek yogurt
liquid stevia to taste
1 ½ cups mascarpone cheese

1 ½ cups blueberries and raspberries
1 cup toasted pecans

DIRECTIONS

Mix the yogurt, stevia, and mascarpone in a bowl until evenly combined. Divide the mixture into 4 bowls, share the berries and pecans on top of the cream. Serve the dessert immediately.

NUTRITIONAL INFO PER SERVING: Calories 480, Fat 40g, Net Carbs 5g, Protein 20g

Walnut Cookies

Ready in about: 25 minutes | Serves: 12

INGREDIENTS

1 egg
2 cups ground pecans
¼ cup sweetener

½ tsp baking soda
1 tbsp butter
20 walnuts halves

DIRECTIONS

Preheat the oven to 350ºF. Mix the ingredients, except the walnuts, until combined. Make 20 balls out of the mixture and press them with your thumb onto a lined cookie sheet. Top each cookie with a walnut half. Bake for about 12 minutes.

NUTRITIONAL INFO PER SERVING: Calories 101, Fat: 11g, Net Carbs: 0.6g, Protein: 1.6g

Raspberry Sorbet

Ready in about: 3 minutes | Serves: 1

INGREDIENTS

¼ tsp vanilla extract
1 packet gelatine, without sugar
1 tbsp heavy whipping cream
¼ cup boiling water

2 tbsp mashed raspberries
1 ½ cups crushed Ice
¼ cup cold water

DIRECTIONS

Combine the gelatin and boiling water, until completely dissolved; then transfer to a blender. Add the remaining ingredients. Blend until smooth and freeze for at least 2 hours.

NUTRITIONAL INFO PER SERVING: Calories 173, Fat: 10g, Net Carbs: 3.7g, Protein: 4g

Creamy Coconut Kiwi Drink

Ready in about: 3 minutes | Serves: 4

INGREDIENTS

6 kiwis, pulp scooped
3 tbsp erythritol or to taste
3 cups unsweetened coconut milk

2 cups coconut cream
7 ice cubes

DIRECTIONS

In a blender, process the kiwi, erythritol, milk, cream, and ice cubes until smooth, about 3 minutes. Pour into four serving glasses, garnish with mint leaves, and serve.

NUTRITIONAL INFO PER SERVING: Calories 425, Fat 38g, Net Carbs 1g, Protein 16g

Berry Merry

Ready in about: 6 minutes | Serves: 4

INGREDIENTS

1 ½ cups blackberries
1 cup strawberries + extra for garnishing
1 cup blueberries

2 small beets, peeled and chopped
2/3 cup ice cubes
1 lime, juiced

DIRECTIONS

For the extra strawberries for garnishing, make a single deep cut on their sides; set aside.

Add the blackberries, strawberries, blueberries, beet, and ice into the smoothie maker and blend the ingredients at high speed until smooth and frothy, for about 60 seconds.

Add the lime juice, and puree further for 30 seconds. Pour the drink into tall smoothie glasses, fix the reserved strawberries on each glass rim, stick a straw in, and serve the drink immediately.

NUTRITIONAL INFO PER SERVING: Calories 83, Fat 3g, Net Carbs 8g, Protein 2.7g

Cinnamon Cookies

Ready in about: 25 minutes | Serves: 4

INGREDIENTS

2 cups almond flour
½ tsp baking soda
¾ cup sweetener

½ cup butter, softened
A pinch of salt

Coating:

2 tbsp erythritol sweetener

1 tsp cinnamon

DIRECTIONS

Preheat your oven to 350ºF. Combine all cookie ingredients in a bowl. Make 16 balls out of the mixture and flatten them with hands. Combine the cinnamon and erythritol. Dip the cookies in the cinnamon mixture and arrange them on a lined cookie sheet. Cook for 15 minutes, until crispy.

NUTRITIONAL INFO PER SERVING: Calories 131, Fat: 13g, Net Carbs: 1.5g, Protein: 3g

14-DAY MEAL PLAN TO LOSE UP TO 20 POUNDS

Drink 7 to 9 glasses of water daily

Day	Breakfast	Lunch	Dinner	Dessert/ Snacks	Kkal
1	Morning Coconut Smoothie	Bacon Wrapped Chicken with Grilled Asparagus	Party Bacon and Pistacchio Balls (4)	Walnut Cookies (4)	1,703
2	Duo-Cheese Chicken Bake (2)	Peanut Butter Pork Stir-fry	Sushi Shrimp Rolls (2)	Cinnamon Cookies (2)	1,705
3	Egg Tofu Scramble with Kale & Mushrooms	Bacon & Eggplant Boats	Spicy Sea Bass with Hazelnuts	Peanut Butter Ice Cream	1,732
4	Sausage & Squash Omelet with Swiss Chard	Italian-Style Chicken Wraps (2)	Sushi Shrimp Rolls (4)	Lemon Cheesecake Mousse	1,795
5	Spicy Egg Muffins with Bacon & Cheese	Grilled Cheese The Keto Way	Italian-Style Chicken Wraps (2) + Crispy Bacon Salad with Mozzarella & Tomato	Peanut Butter Ice Cream	1,853
6	Avocado and Kale Eggs	Beef Cotija Cheeseburger	Vegan Mushroom Pizza	Almond Butter Fat Bombs (4)	1,725
7	Fontina Cheese and Chorizo Waffles	Thyme & Wild Mushroom Soup	Adobo Beef Fajitas (2)	Coconut Fat Bombs (2)	1,707

8	Creamy Coconut Kiwi Drink	Grilled Cheese The Keto Way	Yummy Chicken Nuggets	Lemon Cheesecake Mousse	1,688
9	Quick Blue Cheese Omelet	Ham & Egg Mug Cups (2)	Strawberry Salad with Spinach, Cheese & Almonds	Chocolate Chip Cookies (2)	1,880
10	Creamy Coconut Kiwi Drink	Chicken & Squash Traybake	Pork Nachos + Red Cabbage Tilapia Taco Bowl	Raspberry Sorbet	1,711
11	Chorizo and Mozzarella Omelet	Coconut Chicken Soup	Parmesan Fish Bake	Mixed Berry Nuts Mascarpone Bowl	1,689
12	Mixed Berry Nuts Mascarpone Bowl	Devilled Eggs with Sriracha Mayo	Chicken & Squash Traybake + Chorizo Egg Balls (2)	Strawberry Vanilla Shake	1.721
13	Morning Coconut Smoothie	Duck & Vegetable Casserole	Parmesan Fish Bake + Shrimp with Avocado & Cauli Salad	Parmesan Crackers with Guacamole (2)	1,785
14	Avocado and Kale Eggs	Coconut, Green Beans, and Shrimp Curry Soup	Duck & Vegetable Casserole	Chocolate Chip Cookies (2)	1,712

Made in the USA
San Bernardino, CA
09 April 2019